HOW TO
BEAT THE
ODDS

from A *to* Z

LYNNE L. JASAMES MBA

FOREWORD BY PATRICK "GHOST GOD" CLARK II

This book was inspired by all the people that have asked me how I became successful knowing the trauma I have experienced and challenges I have faced.

Author's Disclaimer: Where quotes are used credit was given to the known originator of the quote. Due to various Internet sites, blogs and quote users, an unknown quote's originator may have been unable to be identified.

For more information, contact the author at:
www.lynnejasames.com
lynnejasames@gmail.com

When you can acknowledge your past behaviors, demonstrate your present intentions with confidence; you can look forward to a future of courage without fear or regret.

~Lynne L. Jasames

Dedication:

This book is dedicated to those who are willing to let their light shine despite feeling as if they are in darkness.

This book is also dedicated to those who are willing to help others while knowing they themselves need help.

And last but not least, this book is dedicated to those who are constantly and intentionally seeking ways to become better to help somebody else.

Let's honor every odd you beat!

Table of Contents

Acknowledgements:

I thank God for spirit, faith, belief, knowledge, wisdom, courage, peace, mercy, grace, growth, the universe, purpose, energy and my perfect mind and health. I am able to give back to a world from which I was able to breathe life into my dreams of wanting to help people see the power they have within themselves to beat the odds.

I am so grateful for the love from my children. I have looked into their eyes and hearts and gained strength at times when I wanted to give up. Because of them I can never give up on being a better woman every day. We have beaten the odds over and over again in a world that sets limits and boundaries on women, African American women, teen moms, foster children, and young black men growing up in a world filled with negative mindsets and systems designed for us to fail. We beat the odds *together*.

Foreword
Patrick F. Clark II

Youth Advisor, Certified Life Coach, Speaker, Entrepreneur, Thought Leader, and Founder of *Supporting Underprivileged Americans: SUPA INC (501c3)*

"If my mother can work four jobs, I can work ten."
~Ghost God (Patrick F Clark II)

For as long as I can remember, my mother has always wanted the best for my brothers and me. She would spend all of her money and run up her credit cards to give us the best Christmas and birthdays she could. She always tried to give us the best. My mother delivered me at 14 years old but was conscious of knowing she wanted better for her children than she had herself. She told me I would not end up like the other boys in our neighborhood. She did small things that would later have a huge impact on my life. For instance, if I did my homework in sloppy handwriting she would erase my entire paper and make me start over! I remember feeling like she was so mean in those moments. After reflecting, she is the reason I have nice handwriting. She would always try to instill confidence in my brothers and me by telling us how smart and handsome we were, and how we were special and unique. I realized later she was trying her hardest to give us the confidence and love she never received.

While growing up, I never understood why my mother cried so much. I knew it made me feel a sense of wanting to protect her, challenge and fight the things that were making her cry. Watching tears drop from her eyes caused a lot of anger inside of me. As I grew up I learned the battles I wanted to help her fight were battles she could only fight herself due to the trauma she suffered growing up. Feeling a sense of helplessness turned into a lot of anger. Since there was no

11

direct person to take it out on, I developed anger towards life and God. At that time, I believed God had dealt my mother a bad hand. The older I got, I started blaming my grandma (her mother) for the pain I saw my mother suffer. Watching my grandma come in the house "skinny as a pole" from being strung out on drugs hurt me! She would stay with us, get back to looking healthy and start to gain weight again. She would start looking presentable just to leave to chase drugs after promising she would never do those things again. I watched my mom wanting love, a relationship and a connection with her mother. I would watch her dreams get shattered and hopes get let down. Her mother made empty promises that made me angry. I hated to see what my grandmother put my mother through. I watched her endure emotional roller coasters continually. My grandmother gave me someone to blame. I grew up with the feeling my grandmother was causing a large part of my mother's pain and suffering. I developed hate towards my grandmother. It also made me lose respect for her. My grandmother became my enemy.

My mother lost her father because he was murdered. My grandmother is a full time drug addict. I understand now why she never felt loved. Not a day goes by I don't ask myself how my mom endured this trauma and has never done drugs. I'm not sure how any person would cope if they lost their father to violence and had to believe their mother would pick drugs over them. I hate that this is my mother's harsh reality.

My mother was molested at such a young age by her "mother's boyfriend." My mother was placed into foster care right after giving birth to me. I know this trauma has caused so many deep-rooted effects on my mother. I believe my mother realized there are many youth and adults with her same issues. This trauma is buried so deep; most people try to block it out as if it didn't happen, only for the pain to surface years later. Having me at 14 years old, I grew up with my mother. I saw her trauma resurface over and over again. I saw her look for love in us, sometimes using her children as a crutch even though we were too young to understand and help her. I saw her self-hatred. I saw her looking for approval to be accepted, loved, welcomed and acknowledged for her pain. I watched her struggle so she used her accomplishments to get through her pain. I saw her looking for someone to give her relief, support and care! Often she looked in the wrong places. I saw her **choose** not to **accept** reality in areas of her life because if she did, it would mean she would have to fit in the box of shame and judgment. She carried that shame and judgment to someday help other people who made similar choices. I watched her struggle with religion. My mother made decisions that didn't settle well with the perception of being loved by God and wanting to live up to "holy standards" that did not bring her peace. She buried her choices deep, because dealing with some of the choices she made would make her believe on some level she was what society and statistics said she was. I remember when I was in the 11th grade and a girl at school with three kids tried to flirt with me. I remember thinking bad and judgmental thoughts about her. That day I realized my mom was that same girl! Knowing how I judged that girl in school put into perspective some of the types of judgments my mom had been going through all her life. Through all this, she always worked hard which I now believe was another way she was able to hide and suppress her issues because she was constantly working. I remember her having four jobs at once! I tell people all the time that's where some of my ambition comes from. I used to say to myself "if my mom could work four jobs, then I could work ten."

My brothers and I grew up and was raised in an environment where people continued the family cycles of drama, pain and trauma. Most turn to drugs or alcohol for comfort, or violence as a cry for help and attention. She **chose** to cry in those moments. She chose education. She chose self-help and personal development. She chose to beat the odds. She chose to stare in the mirror and deal with the person in the mirror and take her head on. She chose to fight and not let her conditions get the best of her. She chose to want more and better for herself and her children. Throughout her life she had always been a giver and has not let her pain and suffering taint her loving, giving heart. Even in her books she gives of herself, her flaws, her poor choices, her shortcomings, her confusion and her humiliation! My mother wants to give others who are sharing similar trauma some insight for their future. Whether you are a foster child, teen mom, a rape victim, a domestic abuse survivor, single parent, raised in poverty or a person with dreams of being an author, a motivational speaker or you want to finish school, this book will help you see that no matter what obstacles you go through, you can do it. All statistics and odds have been against my mother since the day she was born. I believe my mom is "RARE," resilient and has amazing strength. My mother believes that if she can Beat the Odds! So can you! Sending strength, resilience and good vibes to create the energy for you to BEAT THE ODDS!

Introduction

My intentions for writing this book are to bring awareness to core values and beliefs that can positively impact your life, relationships, goals and dreams during the process of growth. I am not saying I have all the answers, but I want to share the things that have helped me be an amazing woman. I say that with confidence. Several times in my life these values and beliefs could have helped me or destroyed me if I was not mindful of my reactions.

Everyone wants their behaviors to be accepted and understood no matter what they do or why they do them. Keep in mind how your behaviors can and will impact others. These energy driven values and beliefs will always match, affect or connect with someone else.

It will take certain methods, tools, values and beliefs in order to stay focused and pursue those strong desires that God has placed upon your heart and in the pit of your stomach. You may have read all about the seven steps, the ten steps, the how to's, the strategies and techniques, and the do's and don'ts to fulfill your dreams and live a wealthy life, but let's not stop there. This book introduces some vital ABC's during your process of growth and development. When you read something, engage in something, or be a part of something if you *intend* to get something out of it, *you will!*

Some challenges will be more difficult than others. The goal is to change how you handle them. How will you respond? Will your character change? Will you grow during the challenge? What will you do differently if the challenge comes again? In what ways will the challenge help you become better? In what ways will you use your core values or beliefs to help the outcome be positive or serve your best interests? *Believe* that every part of your life matters. *Know* all of your

15

behaviors matter. How you respond to things that happen in your life matter. Everything you do builds up and develops into something greater, even the small things.

Throughout my personal journey I have had to turn to many tools, self-help programs, the Bible, techniques, self-help books, messages, videos and guides to remind myself to not give up. I have used these values and beliefs to help focus my thoughts and energies. I have invested thousands and thousands of dollars to make progress to better myself. This progress does not happen overnight. There were times I had to use these values and beliefs in order to not change my character, keep my integrity intact, hold my head high, keep going when I didn't feel like it and rise up in the times when I felt low. I learned what sacrifice, love, and believing in myself felt like, looked like, and the power of all of them. I felt the power of helping others in ways that helped to serve me.

You will be able to identify how to consciously apply these sets of values and beliefs and recognize how they are effective. They are key elements to beat the odds. We ALL are faced with challenges. Incorporate these ABC's to help you beat them!

If any section of this book makes you feel uncomfortable, uneasy, or causes you to reflect on your own life, it's not a personal attack on you. It's an opportunity to evaluate and grow. You may need to acknowledge things in that area of your life you need to change. Make the changes, build on that area, and become a better person. I don't know your story, but we can share in the experience of growing and become better together. Information in different sections of this book may overlap or repeat in various ways; this is designed to increase your understanding and further assist you in applying that specific information to your life.

How to Beat the Odds from A to Z will help you be prepared for the great days when you may feel like taking on the world and conquering every challenge that comes your way, as well as those bad days when you might want to hide under a rock and forget about the world or when you might feel like a failure. Life has a way of taking you from high levels and bringing you back down. You won't conquer these ABC's overnight and not every day but place them in your heart and spirit so when the lows come you are more than prepared to bring yourself back up. These ABC's are another way to beat the lows and get back to the highs without making any decisions that might not serve your best interests. The most frustrating and painful moments in life often lead to the greatest moments. Keep your faith strong, stay prayed up, learn the ABC's to beat the odds and it will be worth it.

Not only will these values and beliefs be tested throughout your journey to help you become a better you, but they will help you become better at serving others. At any moment you can take the opportunity to reverse any past behaviors you want to change or improve. Tests will come so you can measure where you are and determine what area you need to strengthen. A test is not failure or an indication you can't change. This starts the process to determine where you are, and at any moment during interactions you can exercise the change or improvements in your behaviors. This book gives you the opportunity to take responsibility for your behaviors. At some point we all been presented with an opportunity to demonstrate *we can* beat the odds in an appropriate healthy manner and serve others while doing so.

I was not disciplined every day. I didn't have the right attitude all the time. I didn't put forth my best effort all the time. I missed opportunities. I cried over and over about things I couldn't control. I let fear get in the way. I made wrong choices, lost a lot of money and I ran at times when things felt uncomfortable. I beat the odds by learning these ABC's, crying, getting back up, starting over, finding another resource to assist in making me better and I continue to pursue my dreams every day. My dreams include ways that best serves others. I intentionally monitor my behaviors. If I don't get something right, if I respond incorrectly or feel like I've had a bad day, I've learned to counteract it with uplifting reading, videos or writing and pull myself right out of those non-beneficial thoughts and feelings. You can too.

Every truly successful person knows and understands how these values and beliefs impacts their lives and the lives of others. This is not about money, but rather your thoughts, feelings and actions coming together to serve you as well as those around you. Find a balance every day for things that happen in your life whether you can control them or not. Remember to stay in the present. It helps you remove issues from your past and allows no room to worry about the future. Release judgment and blame and stop finding fault within yourself.

I've been asked for years, "Lynne, why are you so cool? How do you remain nice with all the trauma you have been through? Why do you have the attitude you have no matter what?" I had an honest answer every time. But at times my answer changed. Over the years I've realized I am who I am with the love I share and the spirit I have for many reasons. One day I started writing them down. I decided to write down who I am and why I am, to share with people searching to make sense of who they are. As you read each chapter, identify where you are and how each chapter contributes to the person you are. Pay attention to how others see you. Recognize how each one of these chapters affects not only you but also the people that matter to you.

Before you start reading the core values and beliefs in this book to beat the odds, take a moment to think about any situation, action, circumstance or behavior you engaged in that may have chipped away at you. Those behaviors may have brought you down, and how you would reconsider your actions. Is there a situation you play over and over in your head and create scenarios with a better outcome? Some situations are conquered in a day, a week and some a month or a year. The facts are we all engage in behaviors that make us question who we are, why we are here and how we can do better. We ask, *why* did I do it like that, respond like that or realize it was good or not so good in the moment. We wonder what's next in an attempt to bounce back and overcome that moment. We work on bringing ourselves back up to the point our behaviors are healthy. We smile, laugh and cry at the moment we are grateful for the growth we intentionally placed on ourselves. Go beat the odds! There are challenges all around us. I want you to be very prepared and bring awareness to key mindsets and behaviors that can make or break you in any moment, or over time.

Continue to carry great values and have unwavering strengths in your convictions.

~Hombre' Jordan

The greatest discovery of all time is that a person can change his future by merely changing his attitude.

~Oprah Winfrey

It is not your aptitude, but your attitude, that determines your altitude.

~Zig Ziglar

As a football coach, I've witnessed youth kill his or her own spirit due to a bad attitude.

~Donte' Jasames

ATTITUDE is everything

When your attitude is being expressed you have a settled way of thinking or feeling about someone or something in that moment. People have demonstrated their attitude through their behavior. You know, the neck rolling, the hands on the hip or the eye rolling. Your attitude says a lot about you and is a reflection of you. Your attitude is an important part of growth. It's time to take your attitude seriously. Having a positive attitude is powerful. A positive attitude promotes good energy and positive outcomes. The right attitude opens your mind to endless possibilities and impacts the decisions you make.

Don't be in denial about your attitude. Acknowledge if your attitude is not where it needs to be and work hard to change it. The right attitude is not a choice or option, it's necessary. Monitoring your attitude will greatly affect the outcomes when faced with challenges. Your attitude can either draw people towards you or push people away from you. Your attitude towards your life will be a direct connection to life dictating life's attitude towards you. Attitude shapes the life you want. It starts with triggering the right action, which expands what you can do, helps develop the dreams you want to fulfill and helps you believe you can accomplish your dreams. Your attitude can impact your will to act upon your greatness and can create extraordinary results. Attitude at the start of anything will impact its outcome. The higher you go in life the better the attitudes you will encounter. Have an attitude of making people feel needed, wanted, important, appreciated and they will return that same attitude towards you. You can develop your attitude over time through patience if you truly recognize how important your attitude is. Your attitude helps promote you expecting to succeed more than you fail. Having an attitude that reflects "I can have it, I will accomplish it, I will go after it and I will make sure I've earned it" is a part of being successful. Acknowledge if your attitude is negative more than being positive. Examine if you have negative attitudes towards things and people in your life and why. Examine your attitude about where you are right now. Examine what you can change about your attitude. Your attitude is reflected in your relationships, your employment, your daily routine and what you believe about yourself. Even those with good attitudes can always improve. You want a great and positive attitude because you want to make those around you feel great and positive.

Your attitude will boost other people. You get to decide how you will boost them. Think about the time you went somewhere and the person had a bad attitude. Didn't it make you feel some type of way? You won't forget how their attitude made you feel.

One day I was reading my juvenile court paperwork that indicated I tried to run away the first night I was in my foster home. Honestly, I do not remember trying to run away. I tried to figure out why was I running and where was I running to. I remember the attitude I had about my foster home. I was feeling many emotions: anger, gratitude, fear, confusion and relief all at the same time. My attitude focused on gratitude the most. I was grateful for not having to worry about how I was going to eat. I didn't have to worry about how I was going to wash my clothes. I no longer had to worry about the electricity getting turned off. I no longer felt the responsibility of worrying about my mother. I released my responsibility of looking for my mother when she was gone for days at a time. I was no longer feeling stressed about my mother. I started to cry less about the things I couldn't control. I thanked God for the changes that made my life better. I changed my attitude towards the little things about my life, which made me focus on the good things. I focused on what was going right in my life instead of what was going wrong. I didn't know that it was my attitude that made a difference but reflecting back, my attitude made a huge difference. I can only believe going into foster care was part of God's bigger plan for me that I did not understand at the time. I was truly grateful God kept me in the same foster home the entire time I was in foster care. I had moments where I struggled with being a foster child after I learned how society viewed foster children. It became more devastating when I learned of the stigmas and statistics associated with us. It was hard at times and yes, I went through things while I was there, but my attitude served me more than asking, "Why did this happen to me?" I didn't fight my circumstances. I accepted them and kept a positive attitude whenever I could. I had people that wanted to hide my children and me, even take us to another state. I thought about how much I went through before entering the foster system and how it was not worth it to live a life in hiding. I believe God knew I had the right attitude and saw fit for my children and me to stay together. The right attitude made the difference. I didn't want to struggle or be separated from my children, which was always a threat. I heard it all the time: "It's hard to place a teen mother with her baby." It was used as a threat to get me to act a certain way. I know it was because of my attitude about being in foster care that kept me grounded. I did not complain about my life. I spent a lot of the time trying to figure things out, trying to make sense of everything. I have watched many foster youth struggle and reject being in foster care. I have witnessed the trauma children have experienced being in foster care and how their attitude (in some cases) contributed to their struggles. Those that did not fight the rules or reject the changes, and had the right attitude, did much better than the youth that fought against being in foster care. The fight lasted for those that fought against being in foster care until they aged out or went back home, which made life harder and a constant struggle for them. Most of them lived as a runaway a long time before aging out of foster care.

I express having the right attitude towards life because we don't know exactly where our journey will take us. Even when it hurts, God/ the Universe/ Spirit / Energy has a plan and the right attitude can make a difference. I had the attitude that foster care was not a negative or a bad thing, but another part of my journey I had to accept and live through. You will face challenges because of your attitude. Your attitude can influence your outcomes and it's up to you whether they will be positive or negative. I've learned in life that attitude is everything.

What does my attitude say about me?

_____
_____
_____
_____
_____
_____
_____
_____
_____
_____
_____
_____
_____
_____
_____
_____
_____
_____
_____
_____
_____
_____
_____
_____
_____
_____
_____
_____
_____

I beat the odds because I have the right attitude, during the right time, towards the right people. I have the right attitude towards life, my dreams and the things I have experienced. My attitude serves to boost other people.

To be a champ, you have to believe in yourself when nobody else will.

~Sugar Ray Robinson

Working hard is important, but there is something that matters even more-believing in yourself.

~Harry Potter

You become what you believe.

~Oprah Winfrey

BELIEVE in yourself

Believers accept things as truth and they feel sure of it. When you believe you have confidence in the truth, the truth is reality. It's having a solid belief in the truth with no picture. You will have dreams that no one else will understand. Believing in yourself will impact you pursuing those dreams. You must believe in yourself because the journey will seem hard, lonely and unbearable at times. No one else feels the passion you have for anything like YOU! No one else can produce the dream that is designed for you, like YOU! No one else knows that feeling God/ Universe/ Spirit/ Energy has placed in your stomach but YOU! That feeling is real. If you shake that belief off, it comes back stronger. That feeling will haunt you if you continue to ignore it. Many people truly believe in themselves. Their conversation, behaviors and actions reflect what they believe. When you believe in yourself, you think, feel and demonstrate you can do it. Your belief in yourself will have you so determined you will not stop until you find a way to make your dreams come true.

Truly believing in your dreams creates a confidence nobody else will understand. Believing in yourself strengthens the way you think and subconsciously helps your mind develop ways on how to achieve your dreams. You will accomplish some amazing things because you believe in yourself. That belief will create a deep passion. Recognizing your belief in yourself helps you see your value. Your belief in yourself will strengthen your talents, passions and capabilities. Believing in you diminishes doubt, fears, and reservations about accomplishing anything. When you believe in yourself no matter how much time has passed, how much more effort it takes, how much extra hard work it takes, or how much money, your dreams stays alive. Even when the perfect plan fails, your belief will get you back on track. The belief in you will overshadow the unforeseen obstacles and what appears to be daring situations. Belief in you will keep you encouraged in times of doubt. Know that everything you have accomplished and gained in your life is a result of your belief. Hold the belief it's possible and *you can do it*. Forget any and every thought that anybody has ever said about you not being able to accomplish your dreams, including the naysayers and statistics. When you believe in you and your dreams, you visualize them. You will move like your dreams are in motion even if you have not reached your goals, because you clearly believe in them, see them, and feel them.

Your belief in yourself will inspire other people. You get to decide how you will inspire them. Think of a time when you witnessed someone truly believing in something and how witnessing his or her belief made you feel.

I have heard Oprah's story a million times about how she knew what was for her and what was not for her. Even when the challenge was unfavorable, her belief allowed her to move in unknown territory. Even when she was offered a lot of money for a new job she turned it down because she did not believe that was the right decision for her. She listened to what she believed to be the truth for her. Through my journey I have strived for more and believed in myself because I have things in common with Oprah Winfrey that I hold close to my heart. The way she believed in herself helped me stay focused on my own beliefs. I learned that listening and believing in someone else's story can impact you. Taking what I believed about myself and glimpsing into somebody else's life increased my own belief in me, and that belief has led me to feel like I'm not alone. Use any tool you need to increase your beliefs about yourself and your ability to fulfill your dreams. You will face challenges, but the amount of belief you have in yourself can impact how you overcome those challenges. Oprah's stories helped the way I believe in myself because I feel I can relate to her. We both had a child at 14, and both of our children are males. We both overcame sexual abuse and did not allow it to hinder our success or the belief we could not become successful. We both have uncommon names. When you hear Oprah Winfrey, there is no doubt in your mind who she is. Lynne Jasames is just as uncommon as Oprah Winfrey. We both have believed we have a higher calling in this life. When you truly believe in something, that belief never goes away until you fulfill it. We both were born under a unique set of circumstances; she talks about being born under an oak tree to parents who were not in a relationship. Her father wanted to see what was under her mother's poodle skirt. Their energy birthed Oprah Winfrey. I was born under a unique set of circumstances as well. My mother slept with my aunt's boyfriend. My paternal grandmother's exact words were, "Everybody was trying to make sense of how your mother was pregnant by your father. The problem was, he was dating your aunt." Out of that lack of loyalty, I was born. We are meant to be here no matter the circumstances.

Oprah and I think our best thoughts; we get clearer and more creative in or around water. Oprah has said that she will take a bath sometimes just to think more clearly. I've always felt I am connected to water. When I meditate and focus, water always appears, and my tears flow like a river. I can't turn my creative thoughts off when I come out of water. The moment I found out Oprah felt connected to water, my belief about my dreams became stronger. We both believed education was our way out. This belief got me through school without dropping out. Oprah left her hometown to go to school to better herself, and I went to school with the strong belief I would get a good job which helped me earn my bachelor's degree. I wholeheartedly believed I would get a good job if I just got a degree. I was increasing my chances over those without degrees. I had three children before I graduated from high school. The belief I could graduate on time with my senior class is how I actually did it. Yes, there were times when I wanted to give up. I spent a lot of nights crying about what the naysayers said about me, and that made high school even more difficult. Without believing in myself there is no way I could have made it this far. I did not have any credits my ninth-grade year. I gave birth that year. My belief in God is so strong, it increases my belief in myself. There is not anything I have done or will accomplish where God will not see me through. My belief keeps me going because without it at times I will give up. What would make a pregnant seventeen-year-old girl with two children in foster care believe she could finish high school, get two graduate degrees, work for the government for over twenty years, start her own companies, and not give up? I believed I could, so I did.

What do I believe about me?

_____
_____
_____
_____
_____
_____
_____
_____
_____
_____
_____
_____
_____
_____
_____
_____
_____
_____
_____
_____
_____
_____
_____
_____
_____
_____

I beat the odds because I believe when my faith is low. I believe in my dreams when I feel like I want to give up. I believe in my dreams when I don't know how I am going to pursue them. My belief inspires other people.

No matter what the situation, remind yourself- *I have a choice*.

~Deepak Chopra

May your choices reflect your hopes, not your fears.

~Nelson Mandela

You are who you choose to be.

~Kathy Drayton

all **CHOICES** have impact

When you are considering your choices, you are anticipating and relying on decisions that include judging the merits of all the options. You are selecting one or more of the options that give you the most satisfying feeling. We all have made choices whether good or bad we have to live with. It was Eve's choice to bite the apple. It was Adam's choice to bite it with her. The consequence for their choices was greater than what they imagined. Always keep in mind you can control your choices. There will be times when you cannot control the consequences of your choices. Be mindful of the choices you are making or will make, and if they are in the best interest of others as well as yourself. Be mindful if your choices are selfish. Be mindful if you are making a choice at all or if you are allowing life to make choices for you. Your choices can change your life, often dramatically. Your choices can change other people's lives and may have an everlasting impact. Your choices are not always about you. Your choices do not just impact the present moment.

The power of choice is one of the most powerful assets you have been given as an individual. When you make a clear choice, you start to cut off any other possibility. You commit to something and take action. You must be conscious of every choice you make. The little accumulation of choices generates the consequences for the big choices. In some cases, there is no right or wrong choice, just different consequences. You can choose what to focus on, what your choices mean to you and what you will do about the choices you have made. Your choices influence and control your life. I'm sure you have made choices that if they would have been different, you would have a different life. I'm not saying your life would be better, just different. Your choices affect how you live your life, how you spend your money, your relationships and how you spend your time. It is as simple as deciding what you will eat and knowing how it will affect your health. Your choices control your destiny. Through your choices you have the power to change your career, your relationships, your income status, your happiness and so much more. Whatever choice you make will affect your thoughts and feelings. If you choose the wrong person to engage with, you will more than likely have negative feelings and negative thoughts about the relationship based on the choice to engage with that person. Even the choices about what to think and believe about other people will affect the choices you make with them.

You choose what you want to do. You have the freedom to make the right or wrong choice even when the obvious choice is in front of you. Your choices can generate either anxiety or peace. The breakthrough starts to happen when you start to make choices that truly reflect what you want to be doing in life, how you want to treat others, and how you want to live your life.

Think for a moment about when you make decisions about what to do, what path to take, and why you should take that path. How do you make choices about things you are not sure about? How to do you make decisions when the choices aren't very clear? Any choice you make should support the dreams and visions you have. You should seriously process the choice before making it. I'm not referring to the surface stuff here, but the more serious decisions in life. Ask yourself, "How will this impact my life? Will my life be better or worse because of this choice?" You should not make any choice without processing the pros, cons and the outcome whether good or bad. Always consider how your choices will impact other people and those around you. Avoid making spontaneous choices based on your current emotions. Consider what will be the absolute worst thing that could happen if you make that choice. Are you willing to peacefully live with your choice? Can you deal with the consequences of the choice? Make choices with confidence and with a plan of action. Do not look back at any of the other choices; they are gone, done and complete. Looking back at previous choices will make you indecisive and may cause a loss of confidence in the present. Declare that your choices work for you, they are right for you and those connected to you. See what you have learned along the way by the choices you have already made. When you don't make a choice, life may make them for you.

Your choices will affect other people. You get to decide how you will affect them. You may be in the position you are in right now based on a choice someone else made that affected your life forever.

You have a right to make your own choices. Don't forget how your choices can impact other people. You will not control the consequences of those choices in some cases. I made some choices when I was younger that created guilt and negative thinking, after the fact. I was facilitating a training session on *choices* with my clients. One of my clients was talking as if they believed I had never made a choice that had a negative impact on my children because of some decisions that resulted in their children being taken from them. I explained to them not all choices are appropriate just because the outcome does not appear to have a negative consequence. I explained that choices can create guilt and negative thinking because the consequences may have a huge impact on people we love. If you are not able to cope with guilt and negative thinking, your way of coping through it may be inappropriate. My client wanted me to give them an example. I explained how while I was in foster care the threat of getting separated from my oldest son was always an issue. While I was "doing me," I was not worrying about how having a second and third child would impact my children. This was so profound after struggling for

35

years questioning how my mother could allow some of the choices she made impacted my sisters and me. I had to realize in some areas I was no better with my choices than my mother. I had to accept there were times I put my children at risk as well. Even though my outcome was different, it didn't make my choices better. There was always a threat of getting separated from both of my two older sons. Then I had my third son. Again, I was not worried about them when I was "doing me." My choices were about me and I never took out the time to really examine how my choices could have impacted my sons until later. My choices were selfish. I had to own that fact. It made me feel awful. Owning that fact made me focus on making my choices about my children. I wanted to give my children a better life than I had and find the paths that would guarantee I would. I think it's important we understand how much our choices impact the people we love no matter what the outcomes are.

We are living in a generation where people are making selfish choices and not accepting the reality of their consequences and who their choices are going to impact the most. You can learn from your past choices, examine them and make genuine efforts to ensure the safety and well being of others. When you are making certain choices that happen in the moment, they will have long-term consequences. The choices you make today will impact your tomorrow. Be mindful of your choices from this moment moving forward. You have the ability to make powerful and impactful choices that have positive consequences and results for everyone the choices will impact.

I can make all the excuses in the world why I had children so young. I cannot excuse the fact I was not old enough or mature enough to raise them. I cannot make excuses for the pain I caused them due to my choices of being immature and irresponsible.

What choices do I make that impact my life?

_____
_____
_____
_____
_____
_____
_____
_____
_____
_____
_____
_____
_____
_____
_____
_____
_____
_____
_____
_____
_____
_____
_____
_____
_____
_____

I beat the odds because I make choices my friends and family are not making. The choices I make are supported by my actions. The wrong choices won't stop me from moving on to the next choice. I will not fail to make sure my choices do not harm anybody else to make me better. My choices positively affect other people.

Everyone must choose one of the pains: The pain of discipline or the pain of regret.

~Jim Rohn

The price of excellence is discipline. The cost of mediocrity is disappointment.

~William A Ward

Discipline is doing what you hate to do, but nonetheless doing it like you love it.

~Mike Tyson

DISCIPLINE is necessary

When you have discipline you suppress desires that do not fit your needs or your dreams. You train yourself to listen to a code of behavior to correct the lack of your ability to do what may be in your best interest. You are exercising self-control and restraint. You will tell yourself you can't do it, but discipline will make you do it. Discipline helps you to deliberately align your energy with your dreams. Discipline will push you to do the right things and make the right decisions through your actions. Discipline will help you finish projects, take care of your body, eat the right foods, and watch and listen to things that make you better and not just feel good in the moment. There have been many times our laziness, or lack of discipline, has stopped us from doing what needed to be done. When you have discipline, virtually nothing can stop you. Discipline helps you stay focused on your dreams and eliminates those excuses when the dream is not fulfilled.

I'm not just talking about making yourself exercise, eat right or get up when you do not feel like it. Discipline comes down to having a reason, a strong desire to do something or achieve something by sticking to a set of behaviors or code of ethics consistently and over a period of time. It is essentially having a strong desire and being self-motivated to do what seems to be the dreaded things you need to do. Stop and evaluate your ability to control your desires and impulses that do not bring growth. Confront those behaviors that serve immediate gratification. Discipline requires you to commit to long-term gains without falling prey to instant gratification. Discipline helps you develop patience and corrects inappropriate behaviors. Discipline will be needed to adapt to the changing conditions and circumstances you will face. Discipline requires you to be proactive in controlling yourself.

Discipline will effectively shape and align your thoughts and behaviors with your dreams. It empowers you and gives you a greater sense of control over how you feel. You will no longer be easily sidetracked or distracted. Additionally, discipline builds a higher level of tolerance and you will get more done in less time, with less effort. Discipline requires you to ask yourself, "What am I willing to sacrifice to get this done?" Evaluate what discipline can do for you. Discipline does not need anybody rooting for you, pushing you, or getting behind you. You apply discipline because it is in you in all situations.

As a spiritual person I am at peace. I found out two weeks after I had broken off a relationship, the man I broke up with had proposed to somebody else. What made the proposal disrespectful was that he proposed to a woman from the same church we both attended. I was faced with humiliation, shame, hurt, betrayal, self-doubt, anger, pain, confusion, and denial. After the proposal I later found out I was pregnant. I was pregnant during a time when I was attending church regularly, dating a minister, facilitating a mentor program and traveling giving speeches. In this position how could anybody use discipline to control his or her emotions? I was fully aware a lot of people were watching me and wondering how I was going to respond to this situation. Yes, there were days my emotions had their own ideas on how to handle the situation. The discipline I have regarding my character and integrity is what caused me to use discipline during that situation. No one caught me out of character like they expected to.

I had to determine when I found out about the proposal whether I was being told out of pettiness or out of concern for my best interest. I had to keep my repentance to God about not having another abortion. I decided to have my son and not make an emotional decision. Lack of emotional discipline would have had me acting like I needed to prove something when there was no one I needed to prove anything to but my children and myself. There are so many ways I could have handled this situation. I allowed discipline to take charge in spite of how I was feeling.

Lack of discipline would have had me at the wedding standing up objecting, waving my pregnancy test in the air. With no discipline, I would have gone to the church on Sunday or events I knew he would be attending to start drama. Lack of discipline would have had me acting out of character for people that were not worth that energy.

I learned during this process that discipline does not just include a workout schedule, eating right or a daily routine. These things are important as well as disciplining your emotions. I have never allowed anyone to ignite my emotions to cause me to step out of character, especially when it is what is expected. People were waiting to see how I was going to respond to the situation.

I was willing to use discipline and not let my emotions take over. I knew my behavior had to serve my best interests, my children's best interests, all those involved and those watching. Whether true or not I was told many times that I had impacted so many people by the way I responded to that situation without even knowing it. I was simply living by my own code of behavior and ethics.

Les Brown said, "Discipline your emotions or they will use you."

How am I applying discipline in my life?

_____
_____
_____
_____
_____
_____
_____
_____
_____
_____
_____
_____
_____
_____
_____
_____
_____
_____
_____
_____
_____
_____

I beat the odds because through discipline I get up when I don't feel like it. I use discipline to finish projects and save money. I use discipline to read a powerful book instead of watching toxic television. I use discipline to refrain from negative behaviors and eating unhealthy foods.

Success is the sum of small efforts, repeated day in and day out.

~Robert Collier

Enthusiasm is the mother of effort, and without it nothing great was ever achieved.

~Ralph W Emerson

Continuous effort not strength or intelligence is the key to unlocking our potential.

~Winston Churchill

EFFORT manifests outcomes

When you make an effort, you are making a decision in some cases that needs physical or mental steps towards that goal or thing. Effort is doing it, not talking about doing it or saying you are going to get it done. You can accomplish anything when you make an effort to start. Once the effort is made it's easy to keep moving on that path and in that direction. Make an effort to get the idea out of your head and onto paper. Dreams have been developed and started by making an effort. There have been many times we have said we were going to start something but never made the effort. Make an effort and let the first step become a second and third step. The more effort you make, the less fear you will have about pursuing your dreams. If you have already started them, let's make an effort to complete them and remove the excuses for why they are not manifesting. If you have dreams you have completed, then get creative and complete some more dreams. You can understand all the principles of success, you can have your dreams in your mind, say your affirmations and do your visualizations, but ultimately nothing happens if you don't make an effort. You have to act on them. Faith without works is dead. Make an effort to develop, nurture and plan out your dreams.

If someone is beating you to your dreams, beating you to the front of the line, or starting something you were *going to do*, it has everything to do with your effort or lack of. It's not about talent or skill. Effort will get you noticed. Effort is what is inside your mind and in the pit of your stomach. The idea goes from inside your head to physical reality. Think about the feeling you will get when you go out and start something. Before you did it, you hesitated and for a moment you did not want to do it. But you did it! You made an effort. You were

45

willing to be tired, embarrass yourself, miss out on something just to do that thing you've been putting off. Imagine making that effort and giving it your all. The best effort comes with much satisfaction and you will *feel* the victory. Don't give up before you even attempt to conquer that thing that needs your most effort. The effort must be aligned with the decisions and choices you make regarding your goals. You could, for instance, first write down what the dream looks like, that's making an effort. But if that's all you do then your dreams can never be fulfilled because you lack more effort. Effort is always sitting at the table waiting to get up. Make a list of what it will take in small steps to stay on track. Make an effort to check the list on a regular basis to see how much effort and progress you are making.

It was not easy to start writing a book. It was not easy being as transparent as I am now as opposed to when I wrote my first book in 2005. My first book was written out of heartache, pain and drama. I still made an effort to write it. It doesn't matter what prompts you to make the effort. Instead of doing things I would want to take back later, I would silently cry and write. I would be the person that put a man's tires on flat, and then turn right around and pay to fix them. By the time I was done crying and writing I felt better. I released a lot of energy and saw the effort I put into making good decisions. I finally had enough information to write my first book. I had always wanted to write a book. I was a little girl when the first thought came to me. I made no effort towards writing as a little girl. I never even kept a journal. I had ugly handwriting; I was the queen of reading books but writing a book was only a mere thought for a long time. Once I made the effort to start putting my feelings and emotions on paper, the book became a reality. My efforts were met with an abundance of information that later became my book. I had to make the effort and not keep "just thinking" about doing it. I had to make efforts to start making connections, finding resources and keep building myself up. Through effort I started to increase my belief I could complete my book. Effort paved the way to understanding the process of publishing my book. Identify what you want to do, who you need to connect with, how many calls you need to make, how many notes you need to write, how much information you need to research and make an effort to start at some point. Making an effort can be as simple as talking to someone with your same dreams. They can help because they may already be doing what you are making an effort to manifest.

What efforts I am making towards my goals?

_____
_____
_____
_____
_____
_____
_____
_____
_____
_____
_____
_____
_____
_____
_____
_____
_____
_____
_____
_____
_____
_____
_____
_____
_____

I beat the odds because I am making efforts towards my dreams starting now. My efforts link me to opportunities, resources, unimaginable possibilities and meeting some very influential people. I am making an effort to try something different that is connected to my dreams.

It is impossible to live without failing at something, unless you live so cautiously that you might not have lived at all- in which case, you fail by default.

~JK Rowling

Fear is ideal crippling, experience-crushing, success-stalling inhibitor inflicted only by yourself.

~Stephanie Melish

Fear is <u>F</u>alse <u>E</u>vidence <u>A</u>ppearing <u>R</u>eal.

~Unknown

FEAR has no power

When you live in fear you are experiencing or buying into an unreal emotion caused by the belief that someone or something is going to cause you pain or a threat. Nobody wants to believe they are going to fail. Fear makes you believe you will fail before you even try. Nobody wants to admit it matters what others have to say about him or her. Fear of what others might say can be holding you back. You really don't know what others will say unless you do it to overcome that fear. Fear could be why you are not doing what your heart desires. Admit you have fears so you can work on removing them. Face the fear and take away the power fear has in your life. I know people that have videos they want to post but don't because they are afraid of what people might say. They are afraid people might not like the video. Those thoughts come from nothing but fear. You may have books you want to write but don't because you may fear the book may not be good enough. There may be a job you want but won't pursue it because you are afraid you won't get it. Fear is silent and has to be recognized before it can be removed. Fear is fake explanations we create in our own minds that appear real. The more you remove fear from your thoughts, the more confidence you will develop into your thoughts, spirit and subconscious mind.

Take a moment to truly pause and reflect on this powerful piece written by Marianne Williamson: "Our deepest fear is not that we are inadequate. Our deepest fear is that we are powerful beyond measure. It is our light not our darkness that most frightens us. You playing small does not serve the world. There is nothing enlightened about shrinking so that other people won't feel insecure around you. We were all meant to shine as children do. It's not just in some of us, it's in everyone. As we let our own light shine, we subconsciously give other people permission to do the same. As we are liberated from our own fear, our presence automatically liberates others." You have the choice to live your dreams or your fears. Fear limits your thoughts for a bigger and brighter future. It is a product of your imagination. Fear is an interpretation of something that has not happened and believing that interpretation is true. It causes you to fear things that is not in the present and may never exist. Fear is a choice and limits your ability to dream big. One of the biggest reasons most people don't achieve their dreams is because they allow fear to stop them. Fear is normal, but as soon as you experience it, take action by acknowledging it. Don't give fear permission to control you. Fear diminishes your ability to keep dreaming. Fear is immobilizing. Fear blocks you, holds you back and prevents you from doing what you need to do. Everyone is frightened of something. What you fear doing the most is what you need to be doing the most.

Your fears may trigger other people. However, you get to decide how you will trigger them. Think about a time when fear stopped you from doing something, then you realized that fear served no purpose in that situation.

I was sitting in the doctor's office when the doctor said, "Lynne, I have some news for you." I looked at the doctor and almost passed out when he said, "You are pregnant." "What!" I dropped my head and immediately started to feel like I couldn't breathe. I could not believe it. My mind went into high gear with negativity and fear kicked in at the highest level. My eyes watered up and my heart started pounding. I had two children at home, a foster mother, a social worker, a high school counselor and another baby daddy to explain I was pregnant *again*! The fear of not finishing high school, the fear of being separated from my children, the fear of what others would say, the fear of not becoming successful, the fear of not making it with three children on my own, the fear of hearing that my foster mother would not accept another child, the fear of losing the relationships with the two children I already had was overwhelming, and the fear of God being mad at me was in full gear. All those fears drove me crazy. I could not control any of those thoughts. They were thoughts of things that were not happening. The fear felt so real I was in tears and felt immobilized most of the time. The fear gripped me and made me believe those things were *really* going to happen. For nights I cried about the *very real* outcomes of those fears. I did not tell anybody for at least two weeks because nobody could tell me those fears were not real. Nobody could tell me those fears would not be the outcome for my life. I was so scared I couldn't function or think clearly. I believed in those fears like they had power I could not control. Imagine if I did something drastic from believing in things that *seemed* so real. My thoughts were really bad. Those fears lead me to think about doing stupid things. I developed a full proof runaway/ hideaway plan. Those fears could have caused me to do things I could not take back and would have impacted my children. People started to notice something was the same, yet different about me. That familiar look, but it can't be *that* look. The day came the pregnancy was known. I was pregnant and having *another* baby. Yes, there was a chance I would not finish high school. There was a chance I would be separated from my children. People did talk negatively about me. I could have raised my children on welfare and dropped out of school. I could have felt rejection from all the people I was afraid to tell, and from some I did. The relationship with my children got stronger. After my third son was born I figured out bargaining with God did not work and fear was my real issue. I had created the outcome for my life from fear. None of those fears manifested to the point that it caused a significant impact on my life or my children's lives. None of those fears separated me from my children, got me kicked out of my foster home, stopped me from graduating on time with my senior class, getting my master's degree, getting a government job or writing a book. I can say I am glad false evidence that seemed so real lost its power in my life.

What are my fears towards reaching my goals?

_____
_____
_____
_____
_____
_____
_____
_____
_____
_____
_____
_____
_____
_____
_____
_____
_____
_____
_____
_____
_____
_____
_____
_____
_____
_____

I beat the odds because even when I am afraid I do it anyway. I don't allow my fear to overshadow my dreams. I face my fears and know that they won't hold me back. I do not allow fear to dim my light. My lack of fear triggers others to be fearless.

Some of us will never appreciate what we've had until it's gone, then we become depleted trying to regain it. It's best to be grateful for all things that place us where we are destined to go.

~Cory Cabri

Gratitude opens the door to the power, the wisdom, the creativity of the universe.

~Deepak Chopra

Happiness isn't about getting what you want all the time. It's about loving what you have and being grateful for it.

~Unknown

practice **GRATITUDE**

When you are grateful you demonstrate attitudes and behaviors that send a message of being thankful. You are ready to show appreciation and return kindness. The first thought people have when they are faced with identifying what they are grateful for is "I am grateful" but they rarely say what they are grateful for. People don't realize how often they complain and there is no gratitude in complaining. Complaining kills the spirit that brings forth growth. Gratitude keeps you humble and allows your faith to work when there is doubt. Count your blessings before you complain about the things you don't like in your life but can change. If there is something going on that is beyond your control, then that's different. Pray for changes to come and seek refuge in the things you are grateful for within your control.

If people were honest there's not too much we can't control ourselves, we make excuses about not changing them. Gratitude helps you accept where you are and moves you forward to another level of peace and acceptance in your life. There is no progress in complaining, especially if you are not doing anything to change it. If God places you in a particular position I cautiously advise you not to complain about it. The more you practice gratitude, the more you can heal from those things that hold you back or hurt you. Find the time to be grateful for everything in your life, right down to the ground you walk on. Be grateful for the ability to smell and breathe, for new opportunities, for the mental strength to survive and the ability to love. Be grateful for the little things that *seem* insignificant. Think about what you can celebrate and be happy about. You have to *feel* the emotion of being grateful. Being grateful helps you recognize that you are alive. Being alive helps you recognize blessings, the people and the little things that make you happy. Gratitude helps you recognize what it is in life you need to celebrate and creates a positive perspective so you can see the value and good in the things that can't be purchased. Gratitude increases the value of grace, mercy, wisdom, love, kindness, humility, peace, prosperity, a smile, hard times, opened eyes, spirit, strength, courage and the human spirit that is always alive. Gratitude is the key to instant happiness and creates true contentment. To experience gratitude is personal and may diminish the need to feel like you need more. It opens your eyes and heart to see all the wonderful things that are already in your life. When you are grateful you feel like you have enough in your life right where you are. Gratitude helps you be thankful in advance for things that are already yours. It's as simple as being grateful for the wind, your child's smile, seeing someone's beautiful green eyes or recognizing how friendly your neighbor has always been. Gratitude makes you want to give, share, and contribute to all the things that makes you feel fulfilled. Gratitude is energy that allows more to be drawn to you and does not allow you to focus on fear, anger, a bad attitude, negativity or complaints. When you are grateful you can't help but experience the fullness of life.

Your gratitude will spark gratitude in other people. You get to decide how you will spark them. Remember how you felt when you did something that seemed so simple and easy for someone. Remember how you felt about the way the person thanked you.

I started a new job and was excited and grateful for the opportunity. I had to be trained on the graveyard shift because the children would be in bed during those hours. When I started the job, I had a conversation with the person I was training with about how I got the job and how I felt God was blessing me. She opened up and talked extensively about how grateful she was too, the pros and cons of the job, the do's and don'ts, and how she felt God truly blessed her as well. She provided me with a detailed story about how she felt God had helped her get the job and she knew this is where she should be working. I felt truly connected to her story as she told it. I totally related.

She often worked by herself, but I had opportunities to work with her when extra staff was needed. As time went on she started to complain about her job, which often left me feeling confused. Wasn't this the same person who had felt so blessed to get this job? Was there a lesson here for her or me? It got to the point where I did not want to work with her any longer because she complained so much. One day I asked her why she seemed so unhappy. She had totally forgotten the story she had told me about how she felt she got the job. She took the conversation in another direction that was not about being blessed by God. When I asked her why she wouldn't just leave and find employment somewhere else, she admitted it was because it was difficult to find a comparable salary with good benefits.

One day I had to work her shift by myself and found out she was fired. I was shocked because even though she complained all the time, she did her job very well and she rarely called off. When I called her, she was so upset and stated somebody had left something serious on the computer and blamed it on her. She didn't realize it, but she had an abundance of excuses about why she got fired. She did not understand why she got fired. I was really confused because people rarely got fired from this place of employment. As I was explaining the situation to someone else to get some understanding, the response was, "She became ungrateful, so God took the job from her." As I pondered that response I had to admit that made a lot of sense. After that conversation I no longer felt like I didn't understand why she got fired. She lost gratitude for the job. She lost the feeling she had expressed when she thanked God during her testimony. She forgot the reasons she got the job in the first place, and how she was grateful for God helping her get the job. God does things that do not make sense when we lose gratitude for the opportunities He gives us. Gratitude reminds you that you are okay with where you are, especially if you are truly grateful and believe God helped you. Most importantly you are there for a reason.

What am I grateful for?

_____
_____
_____
_____
_____
_____
_____
_____
_____
_____
_____
_____
_____
_____
_____
_____
_____
_____
_____
_____
_____
_____
_____
_____
_____

I beat the odds because my gratitude keeps me realizing how far I have come. My gratitude creates greater experiences and opportunities. When I feel like complaining my gratitude keeps me focused and thankful. I am grateful for the things money can't buy. My gratitude sparks gratitude in others to be more grateful.

I've watched people heal and allow the healing to change their lives. They know the pain existed, but pain no longer controls how they live.

~Magnolia Drew

Instead of saying "I'm damaged, I'm broken, I have trust issues" say "I'm healing, I'm rediscovering myself, I'm starting over."

~Horacio Jones

When you can tell the story and it doesn't bring any pain, you know you've healed.

~Unknown

HEAL you

When you heal, you become sound and healthy and you reduce your stress. You release anger and resentment towards people and things that have caused negative or hurtful experiences. Healing can change the way you view your life in profound ways. You cannot take back or change what has happened. If you are reading this, those things did not destroy you. Your traumatic experiences do not define you. You can take those same experiences and mistakes, learn and grow from them, and accept that they happened. You are not the only person who has made a mistake and experienced something that was either too devastating to think about or too embarrassing to bring back up. There is *healing* in moving past anything you want to change as recent as yesterday. You are not the same person you were when those things happened so let them go. Acknowledge and accept those things and give them no more power to control your thoughts, behaviors or emotions.

As you heal, you are accepting your past experiences and you have learned from them. You are no longer a hostage to the shame, guilt, pain, bitterness or anger that has held you back. Your future happiness is more important than holding onto things you absolutely cannot change from your past. You have decided *the present* defines you, and you can plan for your future, based on who you are and who you will become. As you heal past the pain, success is on the other side. Roads of pain lead to success. Remember, you can't keep talking about the things from which you need to heal. Healing moves you forward and talking about the past keeps you there. When you allow yourself to heal, you are standing up for your future, your dreams, your peace of mind, and better health. It takes courage and faith to let go of things that hurt you. I'm talking about the things that made you cry, frustrated you and make you question and doubt yourself. Do not allow those things you felt ruin you. Focus on healing. There is nothing you can do to change what happened whether on purpose or by a mistake. Those things that left you feeling wounded are over. You may have suffered a loss, been betrayed, taken advantage of, been a victim, or was a perpetrator or the person that kept it a secret. You cannot live, dream, hope, grow, or move forward if you choose to not heal. You will always suffer at some level if that pain, bitterness or anger is still in your stomach or mind. You will never live your best life. The defeat comes when you focus on what was said about you, what happened to you, what you used to do or what you did not do. This is a good one: *what you should have done differently*. Those thoughts destroy your opportunities to feel free. You are in control of your present. Allow your mind to go way down deep, cry hard, let go and heal.

Healing is a choice. You can wake up to your future or live in your past. It's your future you want to pull towards you and grow from. You can hang on to your past and not go anywhere. Both cannot exist. Pastor, author, and filmmaker TD Jakes says "The past has to go, and your fierceness to your future in which you fight determines what happens once you make the decision to heal." When you are looking back you have no energy to build the future that's in front of you. Each moment is a gift and the gift is always present. You can't see what could be if you are constantly looking at what was. Have no guilt about your ability to heal, move forward, grow, make your dreams come true and enjoy every moment in the present. I went through a transition of my own regarding healing. I wanted to be better. I made being better a priority so healing myself from past experiences had to be done. It meant telling people to stop bringing up past incidents that were not relevant to where I was. It meant cutting off people from my past because their attitudes and behaviors opened up old wounds. I had to be willing to be lonely for a while so I could heal from the mental strongholds that were tied to my past. This meant I no longer engaged in any action that would cause me more pain. We know when we are about to enter into a situation that will eventually bring us pain. If not pain, then situations can feel like setbacks. I'm referring to those behaviors we engage in when we are feeling some type of way and then wished we had not done them, such as taking a job for the wrong reason, settling for the wrong partner, getting involved in family issues that are not yours to deal with, having conversations that don't stimulate growth, or spending money that will cause you financial hardships in the long run. I am able to heal from the things that caused me pain because I started making better decisions that protected *me*. I could no longer continue protecting other people's feelings, finances, emotions, and actions. I stopped justifying why people did the things they did towards me and just accepted them. They were no longer my problem. I also had to accept that it was who they were and let go of who I wanted them to be. The same people kept opening up old wounds would continue to do so if I allowed it. I had to realize I don't have to give people the energy to hurt me. I don't owe them a conversation or anything if I'm not in a place of healing. My focus became about what makes *me* happy, not about me adjusting to make someone else happy, or to make his or her circumstances easier. I couldn't heal because I was always willing to lighten someone else's load and wasn't focusing on what was most important me.

Pain comes in so many forms and if you don't recognize what causes the pain or where the pain comes from, you won't heal. The pain, and what causes it, will continue to hurt you. Healing allows you to be honest with yourself and get to the root of the pain even when it hurts. If making changes in my situations or choices regarding the people I chose to surround myself with made me feel whole, then I had to change things for myself. I blocked people on social media, removed contacts from my phone and stopped answering toxic phone calls. I healed because I was willing to admit where the pain was coming from, even when those relationships were close to me.

Oprah and Eckhart Tolle have a very informative video on YouTube entitled "Let Go of Your Past." They talk about a little girl who had come to a very muddy river and she was afraid to cross it. Some monks were passing by, and the leader decided to help the little girl over the muddy water. They picked her up, carried her over, and dropped her off on the other side. They continued on for the next several hours in meditative silence. One of the monks stopped and told the leader he shouldn't have carried the girl because they are not allowed to touch women. The leader told the younger monk they dropped the girl off five hours ago and was surprised he was still carrying the girl five hours later. This is an example of holding onto the past that serves no purpose in our present.

You cannot take back or change what has happened. If you are reading this, those things in the past did not destroy you. Your traumatic experiences do not define you. You can take those same experiences or mistakes, learn and grow from them, and accept they happened. You are not the only person that has made a mistake or experienced something that was either too devastating to think about or too embarrassing to bring back up. There is *healing* in moving past anything you want to change. You are not the same person you were when those things happened so let them go. Acknowledge and accept those things and give it no more power to control your thoughts, behaviors and emotions.

It's amazing how the things you will need will come to you while you are healing. When you heal you open yourself up to the things that bring you peace and take your life to a new level of peace and growth.

What do I need to heal from?

_____
_____
_____
_____
_____
_____
_____
_____
_____
_____
_____
_____
_____
_____
_____
_____
_____
_____
_____
_____
_____
_____
_____
_____
_____
_____
_____
_____

I beat the odds because my pain is not my crutch. I will heal and become stronger, better, wiser and more determined. I put myself in a position to heal from life's experiences and toxic people. I know my healing helps someone else heal.

What you invest your time in defines who you are.

~Todd Duncan

Investing in yourself is the best investment you will ever make. It will not only improve your life, it will improve the lives of those around you.

~Robin S. Sharma

The best investment you can make is always in yourself. It's worth it.

~Unknown

INVEST in yourself

When you make an investment in yourself, you are spending money and/ or time with the expectation of achieving a profit, a possession, personal growth or material rewards. Spending time and money on you is time and money well spent. People spend money on all kinds of things like fast food, shoes, video games or unnecessary products. However, when it comes to taking a training course, spending money on a website, buying business cards or a license, contracting with a graphic designer to promote yourself, paying a marketing/business expert, or attending a personal development class, we rarely do so. Until you decide to put your own money behind YOU, no one else will. It's time to invest time and money in your own goals and dreams. Why would anyone else make that investment unless you were willing to do the same? It's time and money well invested when you are getting to know what you want, what you like and who you are. Slow down and invest some real time and money in yourself.

As you start to invest in yourself, you will see and feel the power of personal growth, which leads to more growth. Investing in yourself opens up your creativity. People that have dreams are creative, they are meant to be creative and that creativity develops when they invest in developing it. Investing in you is not always about money. You have to value your time. Forget about the amount of time you've already spent. Start deciding how you are going to spend your time now. How you spend your time reflects what you are committed to. Instead of going home and sitting in front of the television, take a class at the local community college that pertains to your goals and dreams. Involve yourself with people with similar interests. Spend time reading books or taking on-line courses. You have to spend time every day working on you and your creativity to manifest your dreams. You have the same hours in a day all other successful people have. They are willing to sacrifice their weekends, their nights, their holidays and their time towards investing in themselves. Invest in personal development books by people doing the things you want to be doing.

The time is *now* to invest in you. NOW! Looking busy is not being busy. Make sure your life is not filled with things that drain you and do not serve your purpose. Success wants you as much as you want it. You have to be willing to challenge yourself to see what you can become.

My first investment was the purchase of personal development books. I later started purchasing CDs and DVDs. I attend personal development classes. I pay for my website and the changes that go along with it, as well as for professional photography for my brand and professional editing of my books. The list goes on. By doing these things I connect and meet people that are into and are doing the same things I am. I have been given many opportunities to engage with several celebrities, and my social media reflects that. In fact, Les Brown, one of the world's top motivational speakers, wrote the foreword in one of my books. The more I invested in myself, the better the opportunities I found.

Someone once said to me, "You are always with famous people!" I thought to myself, "I haven't even posted all the pictures I have with a lot of high-profile people I've met!" Another person who saw me in a picture with Beyoncé's father said, "I feel like you are around people that are on the same level as you. You just do not see it yourself." My mouth dropped. I had never looked at myself that way.

Being willing to invest in myself forced me to go further, try harder and believe in myself even more. It also attracted the people that could help me develop and lead me to others that were on my same level, the Les Browns of the world.

What have I invested in myself?

_____
_____
_____
_____
_____
_____
_____
_____
_____
_____
_____
_____
_____
_____
_____
_____
_____
_____
_____
_____
_____
_____
_____
_____
_____
_____

I beat the odds because I invest enough in myself that I get the results I am looking for. I invest my time and money into things that make me better. I invest in myself after taking losses. Investing in myself inspires others to invest in themselves.

The remedy for life's broken pieces is not classes, workshops or books. Don't try to heal the broken pieces, just forgive.

~Iyanla Vanzant

The weak can never forgive. Forgiveness is the attribute of the strong.

~Mahatma Gandhi

Forgiveness is a gift you give yourself.

~Tony Robbins

JUSTICE is forgiveness

Forgiveness releases feelings of anger, hatred or resentment toward others, society as a whole, and circumstances for an offense, flaw, or mistake. Forgiveness is vital to maturing and helps to release any turmoil you may have. It also may bring a sense of justice, relief and power. Alternatively, lack of forgiveness causes us to feel resentful, angry and bitter. This feeling takes a lot of negative energy. Forgiveness must start with you. When you think about what forgiveness means then you can stop those angry and resentful thoughts and feelings. We do more self-damage than we imagine due to the stories and lies we tell ourselves. Nobody has to make us feel shame or guilt if we are making ourselves feel shameful or guilty. When we forgive, we stop blaming others for where we are emotionally. The more you forgive the more you will naturally develop the mindset of feeling justice has been served without the law or retaliation.

If you are not willing to understand the power of forgiveness you are shutting yourself down from true happiness. Forgiveness can release you from those negative interactions and experiences with people and situations from your past. If things are stagnant you may need to search for some unresolved issues surrounding forgiveness. When you forgive it releases thoughts of bitterness, sadness, anger and resentment. Lack of forgiveness blocks good energy, positive thinking, joy and peace from flowing freely in life in the present.

Don't get forgiveness and acceptance confused. There is a difference. Forgiveness is not saying you accept what the person did, the situation, what you did or what happened. You are saying, you will no longer hold on to this pain, anger, shame, guilt or resentment from this particular situation.

In the present moment creativity can open up, dreams can be pursued, and opportunities can come to you. This is where your thoughts and dreams have the most power. Remove the injustice from your past and allow your future to flow. When you blame other people for where you are it diminishes your ability to be creative. Lack of forgiveness diminishes your ability to flourish. People feel the way they feel because they choose to, not because others make them feel that way. We don't have the power over what others do, but we do have the power over our own emotions and what we do with them. You have to be willing to acknowledge you are still placing your responsibility for your feelings onto someone else. You have been given the ability to use your wisdom and insight to no longer react as the same person you were when those things happened. The shame, anger and resentment stops here and now in this present moment. You no longer have to beat the other person up or yourself up (in your head and heart) for what happened. When you let that huge burden go, you open up to what life has to offer.

Author, James A. Ray said it best on an Oprah episode about the best-selling book, *The Secret*. "Not being willing to forgive is like drinking poison but hoping the other person will die."

Listen to India Arie's song, "Forgiveness". It really reflects on how influential people chose to forgive when they were placed in positions where justice was not served.

One day I was balled up on my bed in a fetal position. I was feeling ashamed, empty and guilty about a huge decision I had made. I knew it was for the best, but I was agonizing over it. I felt like I was going crazy. I started destroying myself with negative thoughts and feelings. I felt lost, and felt like God was never going to forgive me. I felt like I was destined for a life of misery, but somehow I managed to live with my decision. I ignored my thoughts and feelings about it, as if it didn't happen. It was too painful to think about.

Years later I found myself thinking about that decision more and more and I realized I was having a hard time accepting it. I needed to forgive myself. Once this realization came, the tears would not stop. I allowed myself to cry and feel that pain. I was hurting from a deep place. I started to clearly process my decision. I had to find a way to accept what I had done. I allowed myself to be okay with the decision. I found forgiveness by acknowledging why I made that choice. I did it and there was no turning back. I told myself I will be okay. I needed to stop judging, shaming and persecuting myself. No one had to do it for me because I was doing it to myself. I was dogging myself out. After I had a painful cry, screamed to the top of my lungs, asked God to forgive me for what felt like a million times, I decided to forgive myself. Only then did I realize God would give me the peace and the feeling of forgiveness I needed to feel justified in my decision.

I will repeat this again. I am no longer in pain from that decision. I can think about that decision without getting upset, crying or shutting down. I allowed myself to feel the emotions I was running from. I faced that decision. I cried a painful gut-wrenching cry until I felt relief. I felt justified in my decision once I forgave myself, and only then did I *feel* God forgave me.

Who do I need to forgive and why?

_____
_____
_____
_____
_____
_____
_____
_____
_____
_____
_____
_____
_____
_____
_____
_____
_____
_____
_____
_____
_____
_____
_____
_____

I beat the odds because I genuinely forgive those that have caused me emotional and physical pain. I forgive those that I feel owe me something. I recognize the need to forgive myself.

Strength grows in the moments when you think you can't go on, but you keep going anyway.

~Unknown

We got turned down, we failed, had set backs, had to start over a lot of times. But we kept going at it. In anybody's case that's always the distinguishing factor.

~Nipsey Hussle (Ermias Asghedom)

If you can't fly, then run, if you can't run, then walk. If you can't walk, then crawl, but by all means, keep moving.

~Dr. Martin Luther King

KEEP going

When you keep going, you have decided you will survive through all difficult situations no matter what. Yes, you will feel like giving up at times. Yes, you will get tired. Yes, your money may get low. People may not support you like you thought they should. Time will pass and things may not get completed. No, the light will not always be bright. You will get frustrated. You will not be focused all the time. Life will happen on this journey and so will set backs. Dreams are not options, so you have to keep going no matter what. When you ignore or put your goals and dreams off they will come back stronger, they do not go away. Be proactive in keeping your goals and dreams alive regardless of how long it takes you to finish them. I've learned I'm on God's time not anyone else's, so I keep going.

Don't mistake setbacks for failure. Setbacks are a part of the process. Setbacks are fuel for wisdom and strength. At times, life will feel like it's knocking you down but it's important to take these as opportunities to learn. Setbacks just mean those things did not work for you at that particular time. There are steps to take, mountains to climb, and a setback is a stepping stone to get you to the next level. Setbacks are opportunities to learn from so that we can move ahead in another direction.

When you keep going, you are making a statement. "I'm going to show up every day." Motivational speaker and author Eric Thomas stated, "I've got a show up rule. You can pretend you care but you can't pretend you are there. You can only be there if you show up." Develop the mindset now that no matter what, you are going to keep going. When you keep going you develop the skills you need. The people that will support you will show up, the resources you require will be there and opportunities will respond to your persistence. Success is the ability to keep going and going and going when your goal seems insurmountable. This is not about potential but your resiliency, perseverance and determination. Think about who or what motivates you.

Your willingness to keeping going will strengthen other people. You get to decide how you will strengthen them. There were moments when things did not work out. Remember the feeling you had when you kept going through the storm? You may look back now and it may not be as painful as it once was.

After ending a toxic relationship, I found myself reading and crying quite a bit. The reading and crying weren't working to kill the pain, so I learned to tap into my ability to write to work through how I was feeling. I published my first book in 2005, and now have written over seven books that are ready to be published. After nights of crying and writing I realized I had a substantial amount of pain written out. One day I stopped writing without realizing it. Life had happened and my desire to write was calling me. I would try to ignore it. At times I got discouraged due to negative thinking and a lot of self-doubt kicked in about my writing skills. My first book wasn't as successful as I thought it would be, and I felt defeated. However, I still yearned to write. I would make notes here and there with no clear vision, but I kept at it.

I started a mentorship program that went four weeks past the expected end date with an amazing group of young ladies who believed in me. Most of us were attending church every Sunday and were very involved in the church. I was in a relationship with one of the ministers and got pregnant. It was a high-risk pregnancy. I was ordered off work and on bedrest for the duration of my pregnancy. I felt lost and confused most of the time while on leave, and the minister and I were no longer together. I felt so many painful thoughts and feelings during that time. My pride, respect and dignity hit rock bottom. I felt humiliated. Somehow, I managed to get back on track and found a way to keep going. My desire to pursue the things prior to all of this kicked in. The yearning to write came back strong. I couldn't quit. The journey was long but when the next desire to write came back, I did not give up.

I wrote two books in 2015 and published one. After my last son was born I further developed my speaking platforms. I went on to create my own fragrance line. I made connections with some amazing people to help me be my best. I kept going. I have been disappointed, had failed relationships, was betrayed, taken from and manipulated many times. I keep going. I've invested money that had no return on my investment. I spent money on the wrong people and wrong purchases. I've had websites crash, books rejected, and phone calls not answered or returned. I keep going. I've lost very important phone numbers that I couldn't get back. I've paid money and got no product. I've had no money at times. I've gotten scared when things and people didn't come through. I keep going. I've had speaking engagements cancelled, monies not paid after services were rendered, spent money I didn't have on my goals, and lost over 50 books in the mail and never found. I've flown to other states, spent a lot of money in traveling and did not sell one book. I keep going. I've cried a million tears over this journey, lost and gained a lot of weight, and still, I keep going. I've felt alone and unsupported by people who I thought would support me. People have fallen through at the last minute. I keep going. The crowds have been small, the sales have been low, the engagements have been free, and my extra money has run out. Yet, I keep going. I have childcare issues, no relationship and not much family support. I do things that cause me to stretch myself. I've missed out on major opportunities. I've had emotional setbacks within my family. I have faced major medical issues. I have been told some very negative things that others have said about me. I KEEP GOING!

What motivates me to keep going?

I beat the odds because I keep going even when things are not going according to plan. I keep going when things are falling apart. Even when people don't show up or when resources are not there I keep going. I keep going to help others.

I like to learn stuff; learning makes me smarter than everybody else.

~Semaje' Jasames

Learning is the only thing the mind never exhausts, never fears, and never regrets.

~Leonardo Da Vinci

Education is not the learning of facts, but the training of the mind to think.

~Albert Einstein

LEARN all you can

When you are learning, you gain knowledge by studying, through experience, or by being taught. You must be willing to learn all you can. Go to internet sites, read books and watch videos to become the best at the things that are relative to your goals and dreams. Be willing to take the extra time to learn about your purpose or about yourself. Make it a routine to constantly learn and develop yourself. People who study when it's not mandatory and learn are set apart from those that do it because they have to. Being willing to constantly learn is a new level of being better. Imagine the outcome for committing yourself to self-development and constantly developing your mind. People that are not willing to learn and to further educate themselves will always be behind and will hinder their growth. Learning starts with learning who you are, what you like, what you don't like, what you're good at and not so good at, what triggers you to act, and what stagnates you. Find out what your learning style is, how you study best and what builds your self-confidence. Make no excuses about spending time and money on classes, books, videos, seminars and trainings.

Learning is not just text book learning. We are willing to spend hours (minimum 40 a week) to learn things another company wants to teach us. Let's focus more on learning about what our dreams can teach us. We don't often take the time to learn more about our talents, our passions, and the things that make us better as individuals. Set aside time to learn your own creativeness. We demonstrate how talented we are for other companies all the time. Make a commitment toward your talents on a regular basis. No matter how positive you are, no matter how educated you think you are, there is no way to substitute true competency in what your dreams require you

87

to learn. There may be times when you feel dumb, awkward, and stupid. True knowledge will kick in and destroy those feelings and thoughts. Learning prepares you for those moments. Knowledge kills those thoughts of not feeling good enough or capable enough while building confidence.

I initially did not understand the changes in policies, procedures and practices at my job; I accepted them and worked with the flow. My job has required me to learn in different areas all the time. I am a writer and I have been constantly learning to write for twenty years, not knowing the whole time my writing was connected to my purpose. I haven't been writing in the context I wanted to be writing, but I have written thousands of stories about children and trauma. I got so upset the first time my supervisor wanted to send *me* to a professional writing class. How dare they question my ability to write! I took it personally and felt attacked. I have learned personal development and my job has helped me develop into the woman I am now. My career has given me an opportunity to mold my writing skills and my spirit. I have a passion for what I do, and it's taken me over twenty years to realize that my passion has put me in a place that has developed and challenged me. There were times when I questioned why anybody would want to take calls all day about children being abused or neglected, or deal with the traumatic custody and retaliation issues related to children. A story had to be written about the incidents. I had been writing in the same position for all of those years and finally made the connection. My passion for helping families had me in a position to do what I love. I realized I have been learning, preparing, and growing as a woman. I no longer question why I stayed in the same position for as long as I did. I was doing my passion just on a different level and in a different way. I challenged supervisors while trying not to be subordinate. Through my learning process I've developed certain skills, feelings, and character to prepare me for the next level of my life. Once I realized I was in a learning environment from all perspectives my job became enjoyable again.

What am I learning that helps develop my goals?

_____
_____
_____
_____
_____
_____
_____
_____
_____
_____
_____
_____
_____
_____
_____
_____
_____
_____
_____
_____
_____
_____
_____
_____
_____

I beat the odds because I am willing to learn what I can and accept the areas in which I need improvement. I desire to learn more. I learn how to be better in all areas of my life. I learn all I can to help others learn.

Sometimes all you can do is not think, not wonder, not imagine, not obsess. Just breathe and have faith because miracles do happen.

~Unknown

Miracles start to happen when you give as much energy to your dreams as you do to your fears.

~Richard Wilkins

I've witnessed miracles happen in my life when I believed they would happen.

~Wanda Clark

MIRACLES are real

When you recognize a miracle, you see unexplainable events or actions caused by natural or scientific forces. A miracle is an unusual phenomenon or event that can be seen, felt and is believed to be created or caused by God/life/Spirit or the universe. A miracle can happen at any time, on many different levels and in many forms. Your life can change overnight once a miracle takes place. You can go from one level to a higher level instantly. You have to realize and believe in what one simple miracle can do, as long as it's a miracle. Something has happened to all of us that we would consider a miracle. When you believe in miracles, you believe in dreams, passion and the impossible.

When you've known a person with limited vision, a negative mindset and with little faith start to believe in things they never have, that's a miracle. You watch these people change their minds and perspectives without evidence: that can be perceived as a miracle. We are all born to live with, and through, pain and difficulties. Without the ability to believe in a miracle and hope for miracles we question why we are here. A miracle feels like the sun shining on your face, the wind against your skin, the spark in a fire, the endless water in an ocean, the light in the sky, the air you breathe and the water we drink. We do not know what or how these things come to be, but we know they exist, and we feel them. Being able to see the different shapes of the clouds, the sight of snow, the sun and the rain are all miracles. Be open-minded about the super natural, divine demonstration, the powerful and miraculous manifestation when things happen around you, and to you. I have heard about several miraculous incidents, like when the mother was late to work because her phone rang just as she was rushing out of the house, and she ended up missing the bombing at the Twin Towers on September 11 by mere minutes. Miracles are personal and intentional for you. Believing in miracles opens up and expands the mind to knowing that the impossible, unachievable and unbelievable can be obtained. Miracles are real unexplainable events that you can see and feel. The ability to believe in miracles comes from experience and from within. Miracles are the belief you are destined for greatness and believing you deserve all that the universe has to offer you. The miracles you believe in are the magic you feel for the things you know are coming to change your life. Miracles are seen in unexpected kindness, unreturned services, pure passion and unconditional love. Miracles are people that come into your life to lift you up, fill a need, teach you a lesson and serve to make you better for no reason but to acknowledge you are here. Miracles believe in the impossible and believe there is nothing you can't do, achieve or have. Miracles are seen in you lifting your limitations and accessing your power to be great. A miracle is watching the universe make all the hard work you put in come together, deliver the order and serve your purpose. Miracles are watching you achieve something that others may have thought was impossible. *You* are a miracle.

In Norman Vincent Peale's book, *The Power of Positive Thinking,* there are so many stories about miracles. As I was reading, I had to stop and wonder if they really happened. I had to read the stories a few times before I could embrace them. The book helped me realize that if I expected people to believe in what I thought were miracles, I had to be open and willing to believe in other people's miracles. I'm a walking miracle myself. I have tons of experiences I believe are miracles.

I had a dentist appointment for a root canal. I had rescheduled more than once, then made the appointment for a totally different date and time than I normally would have. I was running late and was dreading that root canal. When I arrived, the nurse agreed to stay and help the dentist because the other assistant who was normally there had to leave.

As I waited, I started reading my book *It's Okay to Cry* to kill time. The nurse came in and asked what I was reading. I told her about some of the details in my book and she started crying, so much so it made me uncomfortable. While we waited for the dentist, we talked about the book and she started sharing what was happening in her life. She was apologizing the whole time, she couldn't stop telling me about her life. She cried and cried as she was talking. I listened, cried with her and totally forgot why I was there. When the dentist came in, we both fell silent.

No one loves a root canal. I can't think of a single person that has ever said they had no problem with getting a root canal. After my procedure was done I couldn't feel a thing. I was confused because I had braced myself for the pain and numbness to bother me for a few hours. I'm telling you to God be the glory it felt like I did not have any work done on my mouth. It was the most amazing feeling after getting a root canal I had ever had. I even wondered if the dentist had really worked on my mouth at all. I felt like it was God's purpose for the changed dates and times. Everything felt divine, like a miracle. That appointment was for me to connect with the nurse, to help her heal.

I gave her my book and within a month I received a letter in the mail (I still have it) from her. In this letter she told me about the major changes she made in her life since reading my book and talking with me. She was in a much better place and the whole time she worked at that office no one knew what she was going through until after meeting me. She felt like God arranged the whole visit and it was about her being healed. She knew for years she couldn't stay in her abusive marriage. Things had to change in her life because she had been thinking about suicide. I can't explain how I left there feeling like I did not have any dental work done on my mouth. I can still feel the chills I got when I left that dental office. A miracle had happened for the both of us.

What do I believe are miracles?

_____
_____
_____
_____
_____
_____
_____
_____
_____
_____
_____
_____
_____
_____
_____
_____
_____
_____
_____
_____
_____
_____
_____
_____
_____
_____
_____
_____

I beat the odds because I understand the power of believing in miracles. I am willing to share how powerful I know miracles are even if they don't make sense to anyone else. I believe in other people's miracles. I believe miracles are real.

Be one who nurtures and builds. Be one who has an understanding and a forgiving heart. Who looks for the best in people? Leave people better than you found them.

~Marvin J. Ashton

I've learned that people will forget what you said, people will forget what you did, but people will never forget how you made them feel.

~Maya Angelou

The quality of your life is the quality of your relationships.

~Tony Robbins

NEVER lose healthy relationships

When you find a healthy relationship, you care for it and encourage its growth and development. You invest the proper time and effort in the relationship to see it grow. You take the time to get to know the person, invest in the person, or learn about the person. You take the time to help them become better. You know they can make you better. Build upon and never lose relationships with friends that talk about your growth, success and ways you can build each other up.

Examine what type of relationships you have at this point in your life. What are your circles of friends focused on? Healthy relationships ensure you will never have to seek love, respect or attention. Healthy relationships are with people that are positive, uplifting and whose opinions you respect and who will respect yours. Having a healthy small circle does not allow room for entertaining negativity or engaging in negative, non-uplifting conversations with people you can't learn from, grow or teach you anything positive. Relationships come in many forms with different types of people. Evaluate the people around you and how they contribute to you becoming a better person.

A healthy relationship will support you through your trials and trauma. Simon Sinek from Ted.com said, "Relationships are built on an accumulation of a lot of little consistent things over time that builds trust and bonds." Intentionally put yourself around people that motivate and encourage you. These people help you to get back up when you are down. These relationships are not toxic. Develop relationships that are full of positivity and bring good energy. It may hurt but eliminating family members may be necessary to stay in positive spirits and stay focused until their energy no longer affects you. You're not cutting them off forever, just until you get yourself into an intentional strong, healthy and positive space.

More importantly, building a relationship with yourself is mandatory to fulfill your dreams. Making sure you take care of yourself mentally and physically allows you to care for someone else. You cannot expect someone else to meet your emotional or physical needs before you are able to meet them. Lisa Nichols said in the movie *The Secret*, "We should show up already great and expect people to celebrate our greatness with us, and not expect them to make us great."

One day I met this "low-key" looking type of guy at a book festival. During the festival there was minimal conversation between us. We would smile at each other here or there. He left early but before he left he gave me his book, a shirt, and a wristband. At some point we took a picture together and exchanged numbers. His energy was positive, and he presented himself with confidence. During our first conversation, I was thrown off because for the first time someone was talking to me in the same way I am often talking to other people. He was giving me advice and talked like he knew I had purpose before I even told him my story or what I was doing. He expanded my ideas and visions of my goals and dreams, and he did not even know me. It felt uncomfortable because I was used to playing the role he was playing. I did not have to do anything but listen and take in the information. I decided after that conversation it couldn't stop there. The more we talked, the more I was educated, uplifted, and encouraged, all by a complete stranger. When I would talk to him it was always about ways I could improve my knowledge about how I *Beat the Odds* and how to grow and develop my brand. He was always willing to explain what he was doing to improve his skills and knowledge and how he developed his own company.

From this whole experience, I learned that developing healthy, positive relationships can happen at any time, but it's more than likely to happen when I'm surrounding myself with people with similar interests. We still have our friendship to this day, and all of our conversations are about our goals, dreams, the next level, ways to do things better, how to overcome challenges and the changes we need to make in our mindsets. That's a relationship to keep, nurture, continue to develop and never lose.

It happens quite often for the people closest to you to not support you. A stranger can come into your life and recognize your worth, provide solid resources, sound advice, and keep you focused. Stay away from the dream killers, the people that have nothing going on but will give you a full story about what you should do, what won't work with no real reasons behind it. It's just a waste of time. Constructive criticism can be damaging coming from the wrong person. Destructive criticism is detrimental from a person with nothing going on but to criticize someone who has recognized the gifts they have to share.

What defines a healthy relationship?

I beat the odds because I recognize the people that lift me up. I am willing to step back from those relationships that take my energy and do not bring out the best in me. I won't settle for a relationship just for the sake of being in one. I never lose healthy relationships because I need support.

In the middle of every difficulty, lies opportunity.

~Albert Einstein

I will create opportunities. I will do the things to manifest one.

~Michael Anderson Jr.

Nothing is worse than missing an opportunity that could have changed our life or someone else's.

~Unknown

OPPORTUNITY is all around you

When seeking opportunity, you are seeking a set of circumstances that makes it possible to do something. Seldom do we recognize opportunities when they present themselves to us. When a neighbor is struggling with their groceries and we look away like we didn't see them, we miss an opportunity to help them. Anytime you are asked to do something it's an opportunity to create a shift in your life, especially if it's something that may seem beneath you. Opportunities come in various ways and it's not just a call to do something we dream about. It's not often people jump at the opportunity to do something for free. Ask yourself what you are willing to do for others without expecting anything in return.

Most of the time opportunity is subtle and right in your face. It's right in front of you and you may not even see it. Maybe it doesn't fit your ideals or come with a bunch of money attached to it. Have the courage to seek opportunities while looking at life as if it is a staircase to take you higher. Every opportunity might not be what you want. It might not look how you envisioned. It may not be what you thought. This way of thinking causes opportunities to get overlooked.

Unfortunately, everyone is not presented the same set of opportunities. We all get a chance to make the best out of the opportunities we are given. It's up to you to seek the opportunities that make you better. Never take an opportunity for granted but take advantage of your opportunities. Take the opportunity to impact the world and be of service to someone else. Opportunity does not always come in the form of getting what you want. See opportunity as a way to help and not be helped.

I attended a personal development training and I started off sitting in the back of the room. Rudy Giuliani, Donald Trump, Susie Orman and other well-known people were facilitating the training. The people I was sitting with were talking to each other, goofing around and not paying attention to the speakers. Unlike them my employer did not pay my way. I had scraped and saved for weeks for this training. I wanted to absorb everything these speakers were teaching. I was not missing out on an opportunity to learn something just because I was sitting with the wrong crowd, so I decided to move. I quickly moved to one of the few remaining available seats, which happened to be at the very front of the room. I was nervous, but I took the seat anyway. The woman seated at the table gave me a look as if I had invaded her space. I normally don't like to sit in the front of a room close to the stage. On this day I did because I felt like something great was going to happen. A friendly looking guy who occupied one of the other seats, smiled at me. During a break he told me he sensed I was different. He explained he was aware I was sitting in the back of the room with "my kind" (people of my race) but decided to sit at the table with "his kind" (people from another race). He stated, "That took guts" and something told him intuitively I possessed something different. It took me a moment to get it but when I did it felt *amazing*. He explained to me his son had shot himself in the face that morning and had serious injuries. He came to the class anyway because he believed there was opportunity in the room. Wow. Here I was having second thoughts because I had paid out of my own pocket. People in my circle were saying I had wasted my money because I wouldn't even get to meet the speakers personally. They were so negative and couldn't understand why I paid so much for this course. I started to put those thoughts behind me after meeting this man.

This man further explained most like-minded people were at this course. Not all of them, but most of them. The talkers at the back of the room were there because their employers paid for them to attend and were there because they had to be, not because they wanted to be. He discretely told me to stay away from them. He explained, "It's always worth the time to stop and take the opportunity to meet people that are willing to sacrifice time and money to better themselves." I enjoyed the conversation and learned a lot about how to put myself where opportunities may be. When the training class was over, he handed me his business card and told me he noticed how many notes I had taken and that also separated me from the "normal" people. He asked me to call him when I had some time because he had an opportunity for me. This well dressed, educated white man turned out to be connected to the television industry. Unfortunately, I was not ready. I had not yet learned about taking opportunities as they came, or the power of being prepared for them as they present themselves. I did learn that opportunity can be everywhere I seek to find it.

What opportunities do I have?

_____
_____
_____
_____
_____
_____
_____
_____
_____
_____
_____
_____
_____
_____
_____
_____
_____
_____
_____
_____
_____
_____
_____
_____
_____
_____

I beat the odds because I prepare for opportunity, I seek opportunity and I go where opportunity is waiting. I learn to embrace opportunity even when it feels uncomfortable or challenges me. I seek opportunities to show others how to seek opportunities for themselves.

If you can't figure out your purpose, figure out your passion. For your passion will lead you right into your purpose.

~Bishop TD Jakes

Purpose moves men beyond themselves, beyond their shortcomings, beyond their failures.

~Joseph Campbell

Those who live with purpose teach us how to love. Those who love with purpose teach us how to live.

~Sarah Breathinach

you have **PURPOSE**

When you are seeking your purpose, you know your purpose is the reason for which something is done or created or for which something exists. It's amazing how once you figure out your purpose you go into autopilot. Your purpose is not just a hobby or something to do. Your purpose will drive you. It's that thing that wakes you up for no reason. Purpose is to be shared and used to help others.

If you don't believe you have a purpose, you may need to remove those things or that person who makes you believe it's not there. Perhaps it's drugs or alcohol, or depression or anxiety. Maybe it's simply being blinded by everyday life and you're not paying attention to you. These distractions (a partner) keep us from our true selves and from sharing what God/life/Spirit/ the universe wants us to do to bring about change.

Give the things you love the time and dedication they need. You will walk with confidence and satisfaction in finding space that allows your light to shine. Your purpose reflects who you are and what you do. Your purpose allows your mind and soul to become one entity combined with the desires from your heart. You have taken all your energy and focused on doing what brings you happiness while knowing you are making a difference in someone else's life. You have to be willing to work on your purpose knowing you will fulfill your dream even when there is no specific assignment at that moment. It's a feeling only you can understand and relate to because your purpose is for you. Everything you experience prepares you to fulfill your purpose with confidence, boldness and power. No one can fulfill your purpose like YOU!

I remember staying up all night writing my books once I made a commitment to them. I could not put them down. I worked on my books day and night even when I was tired and wanted to go to sleep. I would wake up in the middle of the night because I fell asleep writing. I have missed sleep and events just to write. On several occasions, others have mentioned how I smile and get excited when I talk about writing. It changes my energy when I talk about my passion.

I've also been blessed with the opportunity to write book reviews. I've loved writing those reviews because it involved reading and writing. This is how purpose works. My job has required me to write for the past twenty years and I never tied it to my own purpose and destiny until now. While writing this book I got a deeper understanding for why I have been employed at my job for as long as I have. My passion put me in a position to write eight hours a day.

The things I write about are healing and I want to share the things that have made me whole and strong. I want to share the things that make me better, wiser and stronger. My books have allowed me to share my struggles with others so they can see what resiliency, hard work, and dedication realistically looks like. How I did not spiral down too far before I brought myself back up? I may not have been able to define my purpose when I was young, but I knew I had purpose and I did the things it took to pursue them, even if I was not aware of what I was doing.

I remember pouring myself into creating my personal development course. It was like a drug when I started developing it. When it was time to facilitate and promote, everything I needed fell into place. Your true purpose will work with you and develop as you nurture it. It starts with you believing you have purpose.

112

What is my purpose?

I beat the odds because I engage in my purpose and allow my purpose to grow and develop. I continue to work on my purpose even when other people are failing to do their part. I complete projects that express my true purpose. I stand in my purpose because I help others.

Be humble. Be hungry. Always be the hardest worker in the room.

~Dwayne "The Rock" Johnson

The quality of your work, in the long run, is the deciding factor on how much your services are valued in the world.

~Orison S. Marden

Quality means doing it right when no one is looking.

~Henry Ford

QUALITY work pays off

When you are making sure you are doing quality work you are setting a standard that is measured against other things of a similar kind, or the degree of excellence of something. Have you ever heard the saying, "Do everything like you are doing it for yourself?" I hope the quality of work you put into yourself is spread into everything you do. Quality work pays off in the long run and lasts a long time. It can also be viewed as the ability to strengthen one's character.

You must have enough integrity to work hard and do quality work when no one is looking. You have to be willing to go the extra mile when no one else will. When you are in charge, what does your leadership represent about your quality of work? How well are you performing? People who always focus on doing quality work and people with desires to do their best always get the job done while running on full and infinite energy. People who do quality work are always working, thinking, dreaming, expanding and challenging themselves *for* themselves. No one has to motivate them to do it, they motivate themselves. People who do quality work only see the end result, not why they are doing the work or whom they are doing the work for.

When the goal is to produce quality work that should be the only thing that matters. Doing quality work makes you consistent, dedicated, focused, responsible, reliable, dependable and more prepared than anybody else when there are setbacks and disadvantages. The things others see as petty or insignificant are the things that you need to do and challenge yourself to do. Quality work makes you successful. People who do quality work take their work to the next level while sacrificing and being relentless with their ability to work harder than anybody else.

Performing quality work does not come with doubt, reservation, questions or resistance; it involves being willing to work all the time, all day, usually with no days off. It does not matter what type of work you do, what field you are in or what level you have achieved in the work you do. The quality of work stays the same. Quality work takes sacrifice, personal standards, loving the challenge and the grind of it. Quality work involves working through the setbacks and the losses, and the unforeseen things that may happen along the way.

You either want to produce quality work or you don't. It's that simple. Quality work propels you and accelerates you into accomplishing your dreams. Dreams leads to ensuring more quality work to produce and meeting more successful people. Doing quality work all the time ensures if you lost everything you built, you can build it back up again. Quality work can't be taken away and is a very strong attribute to have. Quality not quantity has much more value to the customer or product. When you are doing quality work you are doing the important things first, not just the things that get you ahead. Quality work is doing a few things really well and not a lot of things "just well enough."

I read this story about a carpenter. The carpenter built quality homes most of his life. He was one of the best homebuilders the company had. The carpenter had become a supervisor in a short period of time and was about to retire. Even as a supervisor he continued the quality of work that made the company a success. The managers were preparing for the carpenter to retire but were not looking forward to losing such a good employee. The managers asked the carpenter if he would build one more house before he retired. The carpenter was tired of being a carpenter. He really wanted to say no and was not mentally prepared to build another home. He wanted to supervise projects. He reluctantly agreed to build the house and took the job.

The managers were so happy and told the carpenter he could take his time, build it how he wanted, and he could use the best materials and the best workers the company had. As the carpenter started to build the house he had an attitude about it; he was solely focused on his retirement. As he built the house he did a good job but took shortcuts. He chose a simple floor plan for the house and used cheap materials. He rushed through to completion but made sure he passed every inspection. He focused on finishing the job quickly.

He did a decent job on the house. He was fully aware that the quality of work he had come to expect of himself was just not there. He knew the house was safe but he was feeling conflicted. However, the house was now finished, and he could move on to his retirement.

The managers were so excited and couldn't wait to see the house completely finished. Everyone gathered in the manager's office. The carpenter slightly dropped his head when his manager expressed how he was going to miss such a great employee who exhibited such quality work. The carpenter thought about this being the last house he was ever going to build. He wanted to talk about how he was glad he would be retiring soon but couldn't stop thinking about how he didn't put his best effort into the last house he built.

A short time later, they all stood before the house and the managers looked at the carpenter, smiling with excitement. To the carpenter's surprise, they handed him the keys and presented him the house as a retirement gift.

There may be times when you do not feel like doing quality work. It could be due to troubles at home, financial problems, or life problems that wear us out and make us exhausted. There could be multiple reasons why you do not feel like doing quality work. I have to admit I have had to catch myself several times and step it up when lagging on projects and not performing at my highest level. That's when you have to push yourself to do your best and you will feel how quality works really pays off for you and others.

In what ways am I doing quality work?

I beat the odds because I do quality work even when I do not feel like it. I work just as hard for others as I do for myself. I feel good when I do quality work. My quality work encourages others to do quality work.

It doesn't matter how you get knocked down in life because that's going to happen. All that matters is that you get up.

~Ben Affleck

God made your spirit strong and capable of being resilient to the whirlwinds of life.

~Neil L Anderson

Don't quit. Suffer now and live the rest of your life as a champion.

~Muhammad Ali

stay **RESILIENT**

Being resilient means you can bounce back from tough situations. When you start to feel like giving up is when resiliency will kick in. Resiliency is the ability to keep going when everything seems to be against you, when everything seems to be falling apart. Just when you start to feel like you are giving up, be resilient. Press forward no matter what. No matter how hard things may seem, it is not an option to quit. You are much stronger than you realize. God/ life/ Spirit/ the universe will assist you with the things you can't handle. It is true; most people give up right before the breakthrough. Push yourself as hard as you can. Just when you think you can only climb ten mountains, life forces you to climb twelve and you didn't even know you could. Resiliency is a quality that allows some people to be knocked down by life and come back stronger.

Rather than letting failure and disappointment overcome and drain you, use your strengths and abilities to overcome them. You can always find a way to rise from the pain. When you are resilient, you have a positive attitude, you are optimistic, you can regulate your emotions, and you have the ability to see failure as a form of help. After things have appeared to fall apart, resilient people are blessed with such an outlook on life they are able to change their course and carry on. Resilient people bounce back and keep going. They know they have the power and responsibility to get back up. When it gets hard, then harder, then even harder, you still have to keep pressing your way through. Resiliency outweighs being overcome. Resiliency welcomes the hardest moments and walks through them. Being resilient means you are going to make it no matter what, no matter what you are going through, and you will outlast anything.

Let me start by saying resiliency is physical and mental. Resiliency dives into life. Resiliency will taste the failure but will not eat it. Resiliency has no time to be a victim, no time for feeling sorry for you, no time for weakness and no time for helplessness. Resiliency gets you to where you want to go with no excuses. Resiliency recognizes how to bring out the good in any situation. Resiliency moves you towards what you want and gets you away from what's not helping you get there. Being resilient helps you to identify how much you can endure. Resiliency shows you just how strong and tough you are. Resiliency endures difficult times and weathers all storms. Resiliency doesn't quit because it loves that dream and there is passion behind it. Resiliency gets back up. Resiliency laughs at failure and doesn't look back. Resiliency keeps you on track and proves to you that even when life throws you off, you can deal with it. Resiliency believes life is with you and you can evolve with it.

Resiliency can and will be motivated by your why. The reasons you press forward play a huge part in you coming back stronger and harder over and over again. Your why has to be greater than the failed relationships, the setbacks, the start overs, the changes along the way, the bumps in the road, the no's, the tears, the negative thoughts and the fears. You can't give up and you can't give in. Resiliency is tough, strong, focused, motivated and gets it done.

Being resilient will break through to somebody that needs to feel the energy behind your resilience. You get to decide how you will breakthrough to them. Think about knowing someone else is watching you. Because you keep going, they kept going. They were able to identify and recognize how much strength they truly have.

Resiliency has kept me hopeful and persistent when mentally I wasn't feeling what my insides were telling me. At times my stomach churned to keep going. I can admit I have allowed so many things in life to distract me from my goals and dreams, but somehow I get back on track. I've written three books but haven't released them yet. I've waited years for the illustrations for one of my books, changed my fragrance line three times, changed the image of my brand several times and have gotten into debt pursuing my goals and dreams. I've lost money on projects, and the person I paid did not deliver. I've lost friends, toxic relationships, and sleep along the way. Yet, I continue to keep going and I can't explain why. My resilient nature will not stop. Resiliency for me is that nudge deep down in my stomach.

I felt connected to Will Smith in the movie *The Pursuit of Happyness* because of my ability to be resilient. This movie demonstrates how a person can get back on track and stay focused after being set back over and over again. In the course of the setbacks God/ Life/ Spirit/ the Universe somehow places him in the right place, with the right person, at the right time after he demonstrates resiliency. This movie demonstrates just how being resilient pays off. Will Smith's character did not give up on himself or his son. He cried his way through. He slept in the bathroom if he had to. He continued to stay focused on believing he could achieve something until he achieved it. Sometimes we don't know what that very thing is that gets us going until we stumble upon it. He did not start off pursuing the very thing that brought him the success and happiness he did achieve, and through being resilient he found his way.

When you are resilient you make no excuses, you get back on track and somehow find strength. That's the power in being resilient. Resiliency doesn't allow lack of resources, time, money, or anybody else's opinions stop you. The most powerful connection I feel I have to the movie is that it is based on the real-life story of Chris Gardner. I still feel the emotions and passion displayed in the movie, and I recognize the pain. Every time I get reminded and/or think about what Chris went through, I feel I am ready to bounce back and take on the world.

In what ways am I resilient?

I beat the odds because I am not stopping until I fulfill the dreams I am responsible for delivering. I continue to work on completing the vision God has given me. No matter how many times I feel like quitting, I don't.

You create a path of your own by looking within yourself and listening to your soul, cultivating your own ways of experiencing what's sacred and then practicing it. Practice until you make it a song that sings to you.

~Sue M Kidd

If you don't have a spiritual practice in place when times are good, you can't expect to suddenly develop one during a moment of crisis.

~Doug Coupland

A spiritual practice is a constant battle within, replacing previous negative conditioning or habituation with new positive conditioning.

~Dalai Lama

develop a **SPIRITUAL** practice

When you have a spiritual practice or spiritual discipline you regularly perform actions and activities undertaken for the purpose of inducing spiritual experiences and cultivate spiritual development and awareness. Without a spiritual practice, what source can you call upon for the unimaginable or what could be seen as the impossible to happen? What power source do you have to ignite when the lights seem dim and there appears to be no solution to the problem? What energy source do you cry out to when no one is listening or understanding what is going on with you? Being spiritual is being alive and present. Being spiritual creates a clear vision of your dreams and you can feel them manifesting before they even start to develop.

Having a spiritual practice opens you up for miracles, adds balance, creates joy, increases belief, introduces your all-knowing power, ignites gratitude, develops faith, creates a positive flow of energy sources, increases unexplainable love, ensures peace, develops clear understanding, ensures your greater purpose, and opens you up to your pure awareness of being fully present to all beings and things. Having a spiritual practice can carry you from one dimension in life to higher dimensions in life. Having a spiritual practice helps you to connect with the unconscious levels of life, nature and unlimited power and energy. A spiritual practice helps us ask for and seek true guidance, creates a divine conscious connection, and helps you align with and to source energy. You will be able to tune into what's going on inside and outside of yourself. It allows you to connect with how you feel and how you connect internally. Spiritual practices are unique to us all.

It allows us to discard untruth and untruth naturally falls away. Spirituality helps you discover truth, what is in you, what's available to you and you will recognize you are the truth through spiritual awareness.

Spirituality is being present with your feelings and actions. Spirituality helps you be mindful and less distracted by life's unhealthy events. Prayer is needed as a part of your spiritual practice and meditation ignites the spiritual state you are striving to be in. Seek and read spiritual literature that can help you find out who and what you truly are striving to be. Having a spiritual practice removes you from the chaotic world and helps you stay in a peaceful state of mind and being. The awareness of real and perfect opens up and allows you to be grounded in that truth. Imagine expanding your presence and awareness of all the positive life forces. Spirituality does and will increase your will power. It will bring higher spiritual energies upon you. A spiritual practice will help you be more in touch with who you are through the developmental process while you are working on yourself.

Having a spiritual practice will reinforce someone else's belief. You get to decide how you will reinforce them. You can't shake that feeling of peace when you are still, close your eyes, and say thank you.

This topic is deep, and I really try to avoid tapping into other people's religion or spiritual beliefs. This is a much-needed area to speak upon when you are on a journey and most of the time no one understands your journey but you. It's not about who or what you practice, but whether you are practicing. I can't help but talk about when I was a young girl. I was not afraid to walk places far in the dark or late at night because I *truly* believed God would protect me. Then there were the nights while I was in foster care I spent crying out to God because there was no one else to listen. I would find comfort and peace after I cried. I hope you have some form of spiritual practice that you go to as some form of support. I can only attest to the fact that I need a spiritual practice to survive. Without a spiritual practice I have nothing to believe in, nothing to hope for, no energy source to understand how I'm feeling when I can't explain it. My spiritual practice gives me comfort and strength because I know there is a force greater than man. I know too many things have happened in my life that I can only attribute to my beliefs and my spiritual practices that created the right outcome. I know the odds were against me the day I was born. My mother was on drugs all of my life. I was in foster care. My father died when I was an infant. I had no family support. I had no high school credits the day I gave birth to my oldest son. My ability to accomplish the things I have I attribute to my spiritual practices. I cry, I pray, I meditate, I read spiritual literature, I listen to spiritual music and I speak in tongues when it comes (because who knows if it works or not). I believe in the things I practice which gives me confidence. Is there anything you can think of that you have in place that you truly believe helps you because of something much greater than you? That's your power source. Only you know what that feels like. It's yours to have and call upon when you need to. It's yours to give you comfort and peace when you need it. The most amazing part is, you can feel it. That feeling you get when something goes wrong, but you can feel it's going to go right. That feeling! Feel it, embrace it, call upon it, meditate on it, pray about it, seek it, *it's yours* to seek and use, discover, and believe in. That one place you can go when it feels like you are going to suffocate and drown, but it brings you back. Those places you go when you are crying and after you go there, the tears suddenly stop. Or that place you go when you feel like you are losing your mind and suddenly the feeling leaves. Or when you come up with an answer to something, but you don't know how you got it but you know it's the right answer. THAT!

What is my spiritual practice (s)?

_____
_____
_____
_____
_____
_____
_____
_____
_____
_____
_____
_____
_____
_____
_____
_____
_____
_____
_____
_____
_____
_____
_____
_____
_____
_____
_____

I beat the odds because I take time for myself. I learn ways to feel free and relax. I practice changing my negative thinking and think positively. I learn where my strength comes from and how to manage my time. I learn to protect my mind, body and spirit from harm. I initiate my spiritual practices to reinforce the power of spirituality for others to see and believe.

Transparency is removing the mask and revealing who you really are; it is getting beyond the surface to what is really going on in your heart.

~Kevin Martineau

The lack of transparency results in distrust and a deep sense of insecurity.

~Dalai Lama

Authenticity requires a certain measure of vulnerability, transparency, and integrity.

~Janet Louise Stephenson

TRANSPARENCY helps others

Being transparent is the condition of opening yourself up to others and being willing to be accountable and, in some cases, vulnerable. Your life has meaning and purpose. You never know how your story or the things you share with others may change somebody else's life and have an impact on them. Be willing to share and give someone a chance to not feel alone in their situation. You may have a message of power and strength they need to hear. Your transparency can change a life, prevent a tragedy, or impact someone into changing his or her path for the better.

Your transparency shows people you are not afraid to share your experiences no matter what they are. Failure to be transparent tells others that you are hiding your pain or flaws and that you may be afraid to show your setbacks or failures, not only to them but also to yourself. Transparency removes the shelters, lenses, and filter of being flawless, perfect, without struggle, without pain, without failure and reflects real humanness. It says, "I'm real and I've had my stuff to bear and my cross to carry. I'm like you with all our humanness." Transparency sends a message of connection. Transparency is freedom told from our experiences, truths and perspectives in an energy and purpose driven way. Transparency is bold, it's courageous, it's real, it's different, it's an opportunity, it's personal, and it moves you to another level. When you are transparent, you bare your soul to others by showing your true self. When you are transparent, it allows others to feel comfortable and creates a feeling of trust between you and them.

Being transparent will help somebody else. You get to demonstrate how you will help them. Have you ever listened to someone tell a story, felt connected and drawn in by their raw truth? Remember that feeling of relief knowing you are not the only one going through a particular situation.

When I wrote my first book I was told several times people felt I was telling their story. People related to the things I shared, and they no longer felt alone. I got a phone call from a young man who said he purchased my book for his mother. He had walked into the bookstore and saw the book on the counter. His mother had been crying for days and he was hoping my book would help her. He didn't even read the back of my book, but felt he needed to buy it because of the title, *It's Okay to Cry*. He later noticed his mother was drawn in and could not put the book down; she read it in two days. Once she was done, he noticed she had an extra bounce in her step and seemed a bit stronger.

He thanked me and relayed his mother had not been crying as frequently, and even said his family had noticed a change in her as well. As he related all of this with excitement and relief in his voice, I just took it all in and listened, taking in deep breaths and thanking God as I was reminded my journey has purpose and will create a change in others.

I could go on and on about the stories I've been told from people relating to my book. To have people from different backgrounds, races, ethnicities, social classes, genders, and ages call or write me to say how my story has impacted them, has given me strength. The feeling of being able to help others shift is so powerful.

I get strength from the transparency of others as well. One day I got a call from a wealthy Caucasian man who told me he read my book in two days. He had been home sick and decided to use that time to read. He told me my book was a powerful read. To hear him talk about how he felt certain sections of my book related to and connected to him reminded me why being transparent is so important. He explained how once he remembered the issues he had buried were priceless because the memories were not as painful as before. It reminded him that some people face the same challenges and come out all right, because as bad as things were when he was young, he grew up to be successful. I can honestly say I never saw that call coming. After he called, I knew my first book had the ability to change the lives of any and all people. Never underestimate who your story will impact or cause to change.

One day I got a call from a man (the player type) whom I did not know. During the call he would pause, as if in deep thought. He thought the book was going to be male bashing, but then delved into the areas of the book that impacted him the most. What interested him the most were the ways I had expressed my feelings. He told me if a woman had expressed her feelings to him the way I did in my book, things would have turned out differently. Those words changed him because he realized what women were *trying* to say. They did not express themselves to him like I did in my book. He is positive that's what they were trying to say to him. He said, "You are the most honest person I know." He was excited and felt my book helped change how he relates to women emotionally. He will get to know more about women going forward. He admitted he had lost some good women over the years. He felt he lost these women because he didn't understand how his behaviors were causing these women negative feelings. He didn't want to acknowledge he was causing those feelings.

It was not easy pouring my heart and feelings into a book and sharing my drama, shortcomings, low points, my crisis, broken heart and pain with strangers. It is my true hope and desire to help others. Transparency was not as bad as I convinced myself it would be. I become more and more transparent as times goes on. I'm not ashamed of anything that has happened in my life at this point in my life. I thought when I wrote my first book I was being transparent, but in my second book I went deeper and opened up a lot more.

How can my transparency help others?

I beat the odds because I know the things that have happened to me did not make me a victim. My story can help somebody else not feel alone. I accept who I am. I realize I am not the trauma that has happened in my life. I am transparent knowing I will help somebody else.

Get comfortable being uncomfortable. That's how you break the plateau and reach that next level.

~Chalene Johnson

True success is achieved by stretching oneself, learning to feel comfortable being uncomfortable.

~Ken Poirot

I think goals should never be easy, they should force you to work, even if they are uncomfortable at the time.

~Michael Phelps

being **UNCOMFORTABLE** brings
growth

When you are willing to feel uncomfortable, you are feeling emotional or physical discomfort. You could be feeling uneasy or awkward. You have to be willing to be uncomfortable to enrich your life. Change does not come unless you start feeling uncomfortable because unless you start pushing past your boundaries, you will remain complacent. If we were always feeling good, then who would change because feeling good is a feeling most people chase. Chasing those good feelings have gotten people in some bad situations. Often, we try to escape those uncomfortable feelings that create a shift and help us recognize we need to change something about ourselves.

Seek to get to a place where feeling uncomfortable feels comfortable. Take the time to examine when you are feeling uncomfortable and what it will take to shift how you feel. Don't be resistant to filtering out all the negative things about yourself while examining all the positive things. It will feel uncomfortable but there is growth during the process. Focus on anything you have a passion or desire to do that feels uncomfortable and push yourself to do them anyway. Take yourself to uncomfortable levels you have never taken yourself in everything you do. Start with easy areas of your life so the harder areas will be a natural process. Feeling uncomfortable is a form of stretching yourself to a new zone. You have to be willing to sing off key, draw a crooked line, take a class you feel might be too hard, get up extra early, talk to people you don't know, or run farther. Once you get past feeling uncomfortable about certain things, you may get to a zone that takes less energy to perform. Fighting feeling uncomfortable takes a lot of energy. You can start a new life when you are willing to feel uncomfortable. Feeling uncomfortable is a personal feeling between you and all the ugliness about you, the challenges you face and the obstacles you are afraid to overcome. That comfortable path you are trying to take will not get you where you are trying to go. It takes checking your limits and pressing past your comfort zone. Do that one thing until it's uncomfortable and learn who you are. You will no longer engage in and pursue only the things that make you feel good. Being comfortable will not be enough. The places you want to go, the things you want to have, the opportunities you are seeking will not be found in the comfort zone. You have to push yourself into that zone that feels uncomfortable to get to the next level.

People spend an abundance of time in jobs they are unhappy with all the time. They accept a less than ideal position making good money and their goals and dreams are "temporarily" put on hold, but still, they're excited. They think maybe this is the direction they're meant to take. After all, it's great money, and it seems exciting at first. Then the excitement wears off. They convince themselves to be grateful for the job "God" has blessed them with. It's an amazing opportunity and they roll with it. The nice house and expensive car don't hold the same charm as they used to. They start feeling very uncomfortable. They thought they would find comfort in all those material things they thought they wanted.

One day they realize they are not happy. They lose the desire to go to the well-paying job. There's no passion, and they start feeling stressed and tired. Then they start showing up late. They start calling in sick. They are feeling uncomfortable but don't know why. They start thinking about the things that excite them. They start thinking about the things that would make them happy. They start feeling uncomfortable. They start talking about the things from the past that excited them. They realize they never wanted to be doing that particular job they wasted years doing. They start questioning their decisions and wonder what is next.

God made Joseph uncomfortable in a prison to put him on a throne. He made Daniel lion's food to see him through the fire and made Esther prepare her body and heart to be queen, only to position her to save oppressed people. God put Job in a bad situation to bring him glory. I can't imagine how uncomfortable Job had to be, going through what he went through. God/life/Spirit or the universe uses your discomfort to force you to where you need to be, to do the job you are purposed for. God/life/Spirit or the universe places people in uncomfortable relationships to bring things out for them to pursue their purpose with strength only that relationship can produce. Even the good relationships teach us certain principals, values and beliefs that guide us towards our passions. If you are feeling uncomfortable, embrace it. Change is coming, and you've got to be willing to move. Not everybody is ready and willing to change. For some it's just easier to stay at the high paying job and allow the money, benefits and lifestyle to keep them from their passion. I know the feeling.

I know a man who was pursuing his dreams while working a well-paying job with the government. It wasn't easy to give up a steady paycheck with good benefits to pursue his goals and dreams fulltime. One day he suddenly realized things at his government job had changed. His job duties were changing with no explanation and his co-workers' attitudes towards him were different. Things he had been doing for years became an issue with new management. The changes started to feel uncomfortable in regard to the capacity in which he normally performed his duties. He noticed little things challenged him to practice what he was preaching in his purpose. If co-workers were not performing well and he addressed them as he normally would, their reaction was not the reactions he received in the past. Things got more uncomfortable when he was suspended for the most unrealistic reason anyone could imagine. It appeared management had been building a case against him. What was not clear was why. His work performance was above expectation. He had never received an unsatisfactory performance evaluation and was a dependable employee. His passion was the exact thing he preached, and he was faced with being able to put those words into practice. There was an uncomfortable feeling every day knowing how he really wanted to respond and knowing how he was actually responding to the situation. He chose to be uncomfortable. He focused on practicing what he was preaching and didn't allow the changes to cause him to diminish his character. His passion is about practicing emotional intelligence. He practiced every day until he resigned. He continued to pursue his dreams despite the obstacles he was facing. This man continued to practice what he preached during the uncomfortable moments he was confronted with. Before he realized it, doors for his passion were opening beyond what he had imagined. It was like a test of his will knowing where he came from (the hood/streets/jail) and knowing who he was becoming (an emotionally intelligent man). He walked in those shoes he created and preached about. When one door was closing many other doors were opening. He was willing to allow feeling uncomfortable to be more important than proving something to somebody that did not understand his power, purpose and influence. Being willing to feel uncomfortable put him in a position for others to see him as weak, but he knows he's not weak. Being willing to be uncomfortable put him in a position for others to see him as a punk shall I say, but he knows he's not a punk. Sometimes when you experience feeling uncomfortable to elevate yourself, it may look different to somebody else. Now those very people who tested what he was preaching have to sit back and watch the many doors and opportunities that opened up to him. He no longer has to work a nine to five and he is happy doing what he is passionate about. It was uncomfortable leaving a job he liked to do. He left knowing it was due to hate, lies, and jealousy. He had to hold his head high and practice being in control of his feelings at all times. He never allowed those people to see him sweat even during the times he was feeling uncomfortable.

What makes me feel uncomfortable?

I beat the odds because even when I feel uncomfortable I pursue things that bring me peace. When I feel uncomfortable I make changes. I am willing to feel uncomfortable with cutting people off as I need to. If it doesn't feel right I am going to examine why and not avoid the feelings. I am willing to feel uncomfortable so I can grow into a better person.

I know too many people that will look you in the face and lie; not realizing they left you feeling like you weren't worth the truth. In spite of, you became better.

~Christopher Gordon

The truth may hurt for a little while, but a lie hurts forever.

~Unknown

When our truth is in question because of one lie, then all is questioned even when its truth.

~Nathaniel Richard

be **VERACIOUS** at all times

When you are being veracious, you are being truthful. Our lives can become very busy and overwhelming at times. We want to do the things that feel simple or easy, and at times we just want to get past the moment. Don't add to those frustrations by not being truthful. By being honest, you never have to worry about contradicting yourself or having to clarify those deceits later. People connect with honest people and can often see past the deceit.

Truth needs no defense. When you lie, you are lying to yourself as well. Lying tears down your spirit because YOU are questioning your own truth! How many times have we heard "Tell the truth and it will set you free"? It sounds cliché but it's true.

Lying changes your character and who you really are. The lie becomes your reality and you may lose yourself in that lie. You project how you start to feel about yourself onto other people. That one lie may snowball and become several, and affects your transparency and your integrity. Being truthful starts with acknowledging areas you are not confident in and builds upon that. Being veracious is a light that wants to shine beyond the limits you have set because of the truth it's built on.

Be veracious about the time and dedication you are giving your dreams. There's no rationalization to the truth. You are rationalizing your lies that are just lies. Be veracious about the small lies you tell yourself. It's as simple as telling yourself the things you will start doing tomorrow or telling yourself the things you will change about yourself. It may feel better in the short time to be untruthful to ones self than to be veracious. Lies sound good to some people. They embrace the lies and make them their truth even after they never become reality. People get down on themselves because people are not being veracious to their heart and soul. It stops people from doing their best because of the damage people have caused themselves. You may not even realize you are being untruthful. You are such a liar what you say sounds so good you believe the lie. There is no power in doing or saying something because it sounds good. Be veracious about how much you want to contribute to making this world, people and things around you better. Be honest if you say you want to help because it sound good and feels good saying it. Examine the word excuses. Excuses causes you believe you are being veracious about something. The bottom line is every time you give or make an excuse you are not being veracious. Excuses are lies. That's why excuses are self-damaging and carry long-term effects. Not being veracious allows you to leave your core values and beliefs behind because you can rationalize the excuse why you left them. It's a lie to say you don't have what you need, the time, the assistance, the strength, the ability or the money. When you say you are too busy for your dreams, that's a lie. Stopping the lies is being veracious enough to start making changes. Stop the mental suicide for all the things you were not veracious about. There will come a time when you will have to produce or show your hand and being veracious will get you there. Lying is not putting in the work and time you need to fulfill your dreams.

I had been working as a part-time family services specialist before I was transferred to full-time. I did my best; I was always pleasant and friendly with my co-workers, the community and management. I was just being myself. After numerous attempts to get on full-time, I was getting discouraged. I was training other people for a position I was more than qualified for. I worked in a full-time capacity, was dependable and trustworthy. After so many times of trying to become a full-time employee, I was ready to give up. I had not had any thoughts of becoming full time for a while when my supervisor called me into her office to "talk to me". I was nervous but believed I had not done anything wrong.

My supervisor looked at me and smiled. She started by mentioning the department was aware I had been arrested but didn't think it was an issue because I was never found guilty. I never thought my criminal record would be an issue because I never had any convictions. What was on my record was not pretty, and I had been honest about it from the beginning on my application.

"We know you, Lynne. After all these years of working with you, I feel you have integrity. You are a very honest person and your criminal record is not who this department knows you to be. We trust we are making the right decision to bring you on full-time to the department. We hope you will accept the position." I burst into tears and accepted.

Those four years working part-time (even though they frustrated me at times) gave me the opportunity to demonstrate who I was before management was able to judge me based on a piece of paper. I take pride in my integrity and know my truth will prevail. I know there are times when bad things happen to good people even when they are truthful, but I will always believe the truth brings more peace. It's my opinion that lies kill us on the inside. Lies cause us to question our own truths and cause us to lose and destroy ourselves. They disturb our inner spirit. Veraciousness is acknowledging who you are and where you are right now in the present.

In what ways am I veracious?

_____
_____
_____
_____
_____
_____
_____
_____
_____
_____
_____
_____
_____
_____
_____
_____
_____
_____
_____
_____
_____
_____
_____
_____
_____

I beat the odds because I am veracious about who I am. I am not a liar. I don't live with knowing I lie to people to get what I want. I do not tell a lie that would cause me to gain while causing someone else pain or a loss. I am veracious because I am worthy to be trusted.

Never apologize for having high standards. People who really want to be in your life will rise up to meet them.

~Unknown

Your crown has been bought and paid for. Put it on your head and wear it.

~Dr. Maya Angelou

My momma told me to treat myself with true and respectable value, so other people will see my worth.

~Michael Anderson Jr.

know your **WORTH**

When you know your worth, you know what your time, energy, and service is equivalent to in value. You will not allow anyone or any situation to waste your time. You will no longer waste your time on things or people that do not add to your life. You control your space and the things you want to focus on in your space. If you don't place a value on yourself, nobody else will. If you don't recognize who you are, nobody else will. You have to set the standard.

When others realize and recognize how you treat yourself, they will treat you with the same respect. Your worth is not calculated in just monetary terms. It's the respect, love, and kindness you place upon yourself that helps others realize to not treat you any other way. Your worth can be seen in the time and dedication towards the things you engage in, as well as in the way you spend your time and money. Your worth is seen in how you allow people to treat you.

Knowing your worth is not about charging high prices for your services. The amount of time, money and effort you put in needs to match your compensation. If you are willing to work at a specific rate for two hours but it takes you ten hours, then that is what you will get. Don't complain about what you receive. You have to start taking action to change your value for yourself. You will start to attract the opportunities that meet your value. This gives you the power to control what you define as your worth. You will no longer continue to allow people, business opportunities, and relationships to devalue you by the way they treat you, express themselves to you, and pay you. You have to act, think, and believe in the worth you establish for yourself. People will only see you as you see yourself. Your worth is seen in how you allow people to treat you in the areas of your life that demand a higher-level frequency.

Additionally, your worth is not in your material possessions. If this were the case, if you were to lose any of those material things you feel define you, then you would lose yourself. Your net worth is not your self-worth. Feel good about yourself without the big house, nice car, and those latest greatest gadgets. Don't allow these things to define you. Your worth will never change unless you make it change. Career positions create more influence but not more value. Knowing your worth will include self-awareness. You will have to identify your strengths and weaknesses and own them. Your worth is not about comparing where you are and what you have to others. Knowing your worth is not a reflection of the person that did not value your work, but rather a reflection of you not applying the appropriate compensation that increases the value in your work.

I had given a speech to a group of teens and was feeling a little off because the host had asked me to speak at the last minute. When I arrived, nothing was going according to plan. Not only was I asked at the last minute, but she had asked me to do it for free. I was grateful for the opportunity so I accepted.

When I arrived, I was told the location had changed. I felt all out of sorts. I wasn't given a moment to meditate on my surroundings to get a feel for the energy in the room. I had a moment during the speech where I felt like I had lost my direction because I was not centered and felt out of place. The feeling I had when I left was draining. My emotions were out of order and I felt like I had only made a few connections, and that made me uncomfortable – this was not something I was used to. I felt like I failed.

154

People who respect your time will not ask you to do something at the last minute without compensating you accordingly. The service you provide is not to be treated like it has no value. Once it appears to have no value, everything after that will be facilitated with no value. Another mistake was not allowing myself to mentally prepare adequately or sufficiently. You should always prepare mentally for anything and give it your best. I've taken engagements at the last minute, but never felt like I did after leaving that event. I knew the program could have compensated me, but I didn't require it. Again, finances have nothing to do with making yourself feel less valuable. The time will come when you have to realize you have paid your dues. Why should any other area of the opportunity have substance for me if from the beginning I cheated myself? I can't blame the person who asked because she only did what she thought would benefit her and the program. I should have told myself my time and services deserve some type of compensation. That opportunity taught me to know my worth. I felt I let myself down. I did not leave there feeling like I was powerful or I made a difference. It's about how *you* feel about the opportunity given to you. The youth seemed excited to hear my story. It made them open up more than they had before during other groups. Of course I was told what a great job I did. They bought a few books and gave me some nice accolades, but it's not about what others tell you. It's how you are left feeling when the opportunity is over.

If I had demonstrated my time was valuable and my territory was sacred, things would have flowed differently. The way I was set up to present didn't feel like it was for a person that has been delivering speeches for ten years with a degree. I felt thrown into an open lion's den. The space was too open for such an intimate group. It was hard to control and keep the group focused in the beginning. I love what I do and have proved for over ten years I will do it for free. If I keep putting it out there in the universe I will do it for free, free service is what I will always be providing. It felt amazing being told I made a difference in one of those youths lives months later. I continue to feel like I could have done better, only because I placed no value *on myself* during that opportunity.

Why am I worth it?

_____
_____
_____
_____
_____
_____
_____
_____
_____
_____
_____
_____
_____
_____
_____
_____
_____
_____
_____
_____
_____
_____
_____
_____
_____
_____

I beat the odds because I learn to value myself. I realize where I have sacrificed and put the time in; God never wants me to feel used or devalued. Realizing my worth will help other people learn to value themselves.

Only a humiliated man can insult a woman.

~Marilyn Monroe

Kindness is the language which the deaf can hear and the blind can see.

~Mark Twain

Kindness is when you meet the needs of strangers and you can't stop yourself from helping them.

~Unknown

be **XENODOCHIAL** to everyone

Pronounced *zeena-doh-key-ul*, this strange looking word is an adjective that simply means friendly. It feels good to be nice, and it's an easy thing to do. Being nice stimulates good vibes.

We meet different types of people all the time, for numerous reasons. Always treat strangers with love, kindness and respect. You never know if you will cross their path again. Being xenodochial can be reciprocated and sends out good energy towards strangers you come in contact with every day. Guess what? It's contagious! There are no strangers among us, just friends we haven't met yet.

Friendliness, kindness or being xenodochial is the new next best thing and is catching on these days. Smiling, being sweet, being a chatty person is attractive. It makes the vulnerable, the hypocrites and even the fake respond. When people display bad customer service or are rude for no reason, it makes people feel awkward in any environment. It is a good thing to smile at a stranger and be nice. Showing friendliness is a powerful quality to share and it makes other people happy. Friendliness brings positive energy to the space you are in. Acknowledge others when you pass them or are next to them. People like the cool, smiling person who acknowledges they are there, and they exist. Be willing to make eye contact with other people. Start a friendly conversation. It doesn't have to be anything deep or personal, just small talk. Ask people questions about themselves. Always be approachable because you never know what a person is going through and how they may need you. Make sure your body language shows people can accept you and not be cautious of you. Body language on all levels speaks before something comes out of your mouth. Send positive vibes to others and smile just because. Don't be afraid to invite people you don't know out for lunch or to an event. Make an effort to make others feel comfortable around you. People love to be around real, approachable, fun people. While you are on your journey to fulfilling your dreams, being friendly can either make or break your opportunities. Last but not least, show some interest and respect and *stay off the phone*. It is rude and tells the other person you are not interested in their conversation. It conveys that you are there to waste their time, which is never a great way to start a conversation.

Treating other people in a friendly and xenodochial way will encourage other people to do the same. You get to decide how you will encourage them. Remember the stranger that waved or smiled at you and you waved or smiled back? It just feels good!

I had applied for a housekeeping position at one of the most favorable hotels during my early years. I was so happy because I was done with the Department of Child and Family Services. I had finally got full custody of my children and was done with the foster care system. I was excited and preparing for my new journey. I was so excited I had a job interview. I reached the hotel and felt excited about the idea of working. As I was walking down the hallway, I saw this lady who had a very serious look on her face. I was not sure if I wanted to even look at her. I have to admit she was not the most attractive woman and she gave me a stern look that made me nervous. I started to feel awkward as I was getting closer to her. My first instinct was to look away. I told myself to smile at her. As I walked by her I smiled, and suddenly I felt like giving a quick wave. That felt way too awkward but smiling and waving was what I did. I nervously walked on to my interview. I wanted to look back but was scared.

When I got to the interview, I was shocked. The lady from the hallway was sitting there along with another woman. She was looking at me like I was crazy. I didn't know what to think. I became even more nervous and my right leg started shaking.

After the first interviewer asked me a bunch of questions that took forever, it was her turn to speak. The first thing she said was, "Stop shaking your leg." By then I was ready to run out of the interview. Then in a nice tone she said, "Thank you for the smile." I was so shocked I just sat there and stared at her without saying a word. Then she proceeded to explain people NEVER smile at her. They are either rude or start making fun of her because of her appearance. Then because I waved, she realized there are good strangers in this world. I reminded her to hold her head up higher, with confidence and more often. Her eyes were watery. I started tearing up myself. She said, "It's employees like you that will make our customers come back. You got the job." I started crying and silently thanked God.

Why is being xenodochial important?

I beat the odds because I am xenodochial when I don't have to be.
I am xenodochial because being nice is who I am. I am
xenodichial to encourage others to be kind to strangers.

You have Greatness in YOU!

~Les Brown

You matter! You might be one drop in a bigger ocean, but even that drop causes ripples which affect every other drop.

~Sue Krebs

You matter to somebody in the world. And no matter what you do, that somebody will always be proud of you. So stop cowering in fear of humility and start making your life yours!

~Jacob Dickens

YOU matter

When you know and believe you matter, YOU matter. You were born. You are here. You are breathing. You have your right mind. It's your birthright to be here. You survived the thing you thought you wouldn't overcome. You overcame that one thing you thought would hold you back. At all moments, at any place, regardless of your race or gender, no matter where you are, no matter what team you are on, you matter. What you believe in matters. How you function matters. Who you are matters. What you want to do matters. Your talents, gifts, purpose and passion matters. You have to believe you matter so others can know you matter. The more you believe you matter, the quicker you will embrace your journey and start moving towards the desires of your heart. You were born for a reason and only you can execute why God brought you here. Thousands and thousands of sperm cells didn't survive. *You* made it. You are here because you matter.

Focus on this very moment right now. The current space you are in. Nothing takes away from the fact you are here right now. This means you have an opportunity to share your dreams with others. Lives can be changed and shifted and more love can be given to those that are meant to see the steps you have taken to bring love. Others will embrace you as a blessing. You matter, your story matters, your presence, your gifts and your dreams matter. You matter so begin to walk, talk, believe, and think like you matter.

Motivational speaker, author, and minister Eric Thomas has said this a million times: "You are important, and you are valuable. Look in the mirror at YOU! Who you are matters. Everybody in this thing called life matters. You can change somebody's life believing you matter. You can inspire, encourage, embrace and motivate somebody else. The way you do things matters. You have power. You are whatever you say you are from beautiful to being the president of your world. Manifest the glory of you that is you. You give others the courage and permission to believe they matter. You will never experience life the way you are supposed to until you recognize you matter."

Knowing you matter will encourage other people to know they matter. You get to decide how you will encourage them. Think about the person that usually says negative things about themselves and for some reason you don't see anything negative about them.

I have heard Oprah say many times she is meant to be here. She has talked about being born under a unique set of circumstances because her father wanted to know what was under her mother's poodle skirt. Imagine that. That one encounter and boom, like magic, Oprah was born. Like Oprah's story, my parents were not in love or in a loving relationship. I was not born out of a loving, open, honest or respectful relationship. I was born out of deceit, lies and lack of loyalty. My father was dating my aunt, and he cheated on her with my mother. When I found out, it was a shock and took me a long time to digest. It sounds crazy, messed up and disgraceful but that is the truth. If my mother and father did not commit a selfish act, I wouldn't be here. I matter, and I am meant to be here. I have to scream, "I matter!" out loud from the depths of my soul sometimes to feel it. I can't let how I got here rule how I feel about being here. I have a huge purpose to fulfill to be born under those conditions. Once you truly believe you matter it goes from the mind to the heart and you can truly feel loving you. Until I realized I matter, my self-esteem ruled parts of my life. The fact that I truly started to believe I matter impacted how I started to commit to my goals, purpose and dreams. The fact I was born under a unique set of circumstances clearly indicates I matter, or I wouldn't be here.

Why do I matter?

_____
_____
_____
_____
_____
_____
_____
_____
_____
_____
_____
_____
_____
_____
_____
_____
_____
_____
_____
_____
_____
_____
_____
_____
_____
_____
_____
_____
_____

I beat the odds because out of lack of loyalty a beautiful person was born. I overcame the pain, lies and deceit that were done to create me. I know I am meant to be here. I know I matter to encourage other people to know they matter.

Stay focused on pursuing your dreams. Life can take you from having no vision to a clear vision when you zero in.

~Mary Crystal

Will gives us the ability to take an idea and zero right in on something.

~Bob Proctor

Do not let what you cannot do interfere with what you can do, zero in.

~John Wooden

ZERO in on your dreams

When you zero in on something you are focusing on the things you want and desire. Zero in on your dreams by repeatedly working on them. Focus and meditate on your dreams. Pray about your dreams and make your dreams a part of your everyday thoughts and actions. Breathe and inhale your dreams. Your dreams are yours and nobody else's. Your dreams have your name on them and cannot come to life unless *you* bring them to life. Only you can make your dreams happen. The thing you are destined to do is only for you. Nobody can do what's destined for you, like you can or share your dreams like you.

Treat your dreams like you would when making plans, scheduling an important appointment or finishing a class. You are constantly zeroed in on that particular goal you want to accomplish. When you are planning, your thoughts are centered on that particular goal. You're making calls, you're texting, you're thinking about what's going to happen before you go to sleep and when you wake up. You're imagining the things you will do. You have to zero in on your dreams with a lot of effort and concentration. When you zero in on your dreams, you have decided to follow and pursue them relentlessly. You have reached a point where you are clear about them, what you want to do with them, how you will implement them and what you want to accomplish with them. You have decided to evaluate all options and consciously commit to doing everything you can to work towards making your dreams a reality.

You have to write your dreams down and visualize them. When you write them down it helps to zero in on them and see them clearly. Write down realistic ideas about your dreams that give you confidence. Writing them down will help open your mind to what you might be capable of achieving. Don't underestimate how powerful and relevant what you want to achieve can be. You can start zeroing in on your dreams once you clearly define them and truly recognize they are realistic and obtainable. You will think about making your dreams come true without reservation, hesitation or doubt. Start taking small attainable steps towards your dreams and watch how your soul responds to your calling. When any setback or challenge comes, you will go into autopilot to push through them to stay on track. When you have a setback, use it as a lesson to push forward and draw more strength. The setbacks are a part of recognizing how bad you want to pursue your dreams. The moment will come when you realize you will not allow anything to prevent you from reaching and pursuing your dreams.

Zeroing in on your dreams will motivate others to zero in on their dreams. You get to decide how you will motivate them. Think about a person that is always talking about and working on their dreams. They are always finding something new to do with their dreams. This usually makes me feel some type of way and motivates me to focus on my own dreams.

It took me a long time to really start to make my dreams a part of everything I do. It took coaching, reading, listening and writing to really get me to zero in on my dreams. I dropped the ball on my dreams when I wasn't making them a part of everything I did. It cost me energy, time, and money not zeroing in on my dreams. I lost out on reaching someone that needed to hear my message. I spent days crying and doubting whether I could write another book or be of value to anyone. I had to make my dreams a constant part of my thoughts and make them a priority.

Without zeroing in on my dreams, I failed to produce and failed to complete things that were a part of me fulfilling my dreams. I would get mad when things wouldn't come together. If I was not zeroed in, how could my dreams come together? I would get upset if people failed to complete tasks or produce a product I paid for. The reality is, because I gave the responsibility to someone else, it stopped me from zeroing in on my purpose, ideas, visions, goals and *my* dreams.

I read an old story that truly reflects the importance of zeroing in on your goal. It takes place in ancient India. On this particular day there were several young men being taught archery. The teacher hung a wooden crow from a tree branch. The teacher advised the students to only aim for the crow's eyes as they looked towards the tree. The teacher asked the students what they observed before they took their shot. The first student approached the area and was asked by the teacher, "What do you see?" The student said, "I see the garden, the tree, the flowers, and everything!" The teacher said nothing and asked the student to step aside without taking his shot. He asked the next student, "What do you see?" The next student described the same as the previous student and he too was asked to step aside. Another student described the air and the leaves blowing with the wind. The teacher continued to ask each student the same question and each student gave similar answers.

Finally, one student approached the teacher and was asked, like the others, "What do you see?" The student looked towards the tree, focused his eyes and said, "I can only see the crow's eyes." The teacher turned around to face the other students and triumphantly shouted, "Release your bow!" The student pulled his bow back and smoothly hit the crow right between the eyes.

This story illustrates how important it is to stay focused on the task at hand. Staying zeroed in requires you to remove from your vision all the things that distract you from your goals and dreams. The student kept his eyes on the main goal of hitting that crow between his eyes and was able to zero in on the purpose of the lesson.

What am I doing to zero in on my goals and dreams?

_____
_____
_____
_____
_____
_____
_____
_____
_____
_____
_____
_____
_____
_____
_____
_____
_____
_____
_____
_____
_____
_____
_____
_____
_____
_____

I beat the odds because I make my dreams a part of what I do every day. I zero in because I'm making my dreams a reality. I zero in on my dreams to encourage someone else to zero in on their dreams.

People cry, not because they're weak, but because they have been strong for so long.

~Johnny Depp

When I cry, my tears are my unspoken language that my heart is expressing through energy.

~Lynne L Jasames

Sometimes a good cry is just what you need to release all the hurt you have built up inside.

~C. Villeme

BONUS CHAPTER
Crying is a Coping Skill

When you cry you are expressing an inarticulate sound, while dropping a watery fluid that forms and comes from your eyes. Crying is a way of acknowledging feeling sad, frustrated, pain or anger. Crying is also a way of feeling healed, stronger and happy. There are times a painful cry is needed as well as a joyful cry. Get rid of the idea that crying is a negative or weak attribute. There is strength and power in crying.

I discovered for myself crying is not a weakness but a part of being human. My tears remind me life matters. The ability to be okay with crying pulls from where you are in the moment. It's ok to cry because it is an opportunity to release energy and break through the moment of joy, pain, loss, regret, courage and any other emotion while being in the present. Crying changes how I move through my pain or happiness. I have gained wisdom from crying because I feel peace afterwards.

Spirituality ties all of us together, that non-physical connection between our energy and emotions. Crying is spiritual. Crying connects what's energetically understood between people, a connection that is a physical sign of understanding how we feel while connecting with how someone else feels. Energy transcends through energy channels. The minute I accepted crying was a super power for me, I understood why I cry when things happened to other people I have never met. I understood why the tragedies on the news makes me cry. That universal connection through my tears makes their pain, my pain. Crying is another way to really identify and understand how we are all connected. It is a part of being human for us to cry and feel for one another. Think about why we get emotionally charged at the adulterer, abuser, murder or the rapist. We also get emotionally charged at the amazing singer, dancer, new president and/or game winning shot. That connection is due to our energy between US. That energy creates the connection. We can meet a total stranger and feel a need to get to know them. The vulnerable part is the belief we know the feelings are true and real. Denying that truth is where we've failed to make the connection. Maya Angelou's quote, "I've learned that people will forget what you said, people will forget what you did, but people will never forget how you made them feel" is a true way of realizing the connection between people.

One day I thought long and hard about crying. I went back to the first time I cried. The first time I cried was the confirmation I was alive (the day I was born). If I had not cried the doctor and everyone around would have thought something was wrong with me. So how is it we don't think something is wrong with people that don't cry? How did the power of crying become a weakness? Our tears transcend us from releasing, our awakening, our peace, our breakdowns, our breakthroughs, and acknowledging our truths. The deepness of tears is the essence of human connections and energy transcending a physical message. It is unfortunate people are willing to deny their truth due to fear of the wrong beliefs about crying, especially if they are in an environment that does not welcome tears. I realized I had nothing to lose in that moment if I cried.

Denying our tears is covering up the pain in the moment and shifting the realness of who we are. People can become less connected the less they cry. We set ourselves free when we release the tears right in the moment. If not, we transcend that energy somewhere else and release it in other ways. We deny what holding energy in does to our spiritual being. The energy builds from one moment to the next. That energy becomes someone else's fault and they can become the target of release. Failing to release that energy could manifest in sickness or disease. The buildup of energy causes people to blame life experiences on other people and deny their own pain (the truth). We look at people crying and want them to stop or wish we could take the moment away if we feel it's due to sadness. People that are not connected want the tears to shut down, stop and shift. We can't explain in the moment why, but naturally that energy comes. We feel it! Shutting the tears (energy) down does not fix the energy in that moment. That energy has a need and desire to be released for some healing to come in. People who cry are the healers, do the healing and are awakened to their ability to heal outside of themselves.

As a woman who has spent her entire life unafraid to cry, I have attracted strangers to me that poured their entire life into me and cried the entire time, and I felt it. I owned it and cried with them. I have watched broken people totally change after a good long cry. They have the ability to get back up and never feel the same way. It's usually when they stay in the moment and release the energy. I started intentionally doing the hard ugly cry after I felt people did me wrong. After that cry, they could never impact me the same way ever again. That cry released all sorts of energy that I carried towards that person. Energy I didn't know I had towards them was expressed. I struggled and fought for peace for myself due to beliefs other people placed on me, and beliefs about crying was one of them. There is a culture where the universal message is crying is weak. I fought and struggled with my own truth about crying instead of going with the flow of my own energy. It's worse when you struggle with your own peace and deny your own truth. Recognize your truth is not everybody else's truth; it's what makes us unique and connected. We can have the same values and beliefs, we can relate to the same truths, but OUR individual truths can be different. What you have learned, experienced or was taught about crying reveals the truth about crying for yourself when you embrace the power of your tears. The thought that I, at one point would rather allow the teachings of others to dictate my peace, my freedom from sickness, heartache, fear, confusion and doubt that is instilled in religious practices no longer saddens me. I cried to be awakened and so has my awareness about crying.

I grew to realize and understand people that do not cry are not stronger than the people that are willing to cry and be vulnerable. I am willing to cry and be vulnerable. These attributes have contributed to who I am. Tears have allowed my energy to thrive and be welcomed. I know people that become under and overachievers, have medical issues, have behavioral problems, or engage in drugs or alcohol use because they did not cry in the moment when the energy was there. They failed to release the energy (a way of coping), and their behaviors reflect how the energy was released. Our failure or success comes from acknowledging our pain and our connection to how we truly feel in that moment. The way we release our emotions more often than not dictates what path we choose. People turn to what they think they know is best. They do what makes them feel good in the moment. I turned to crying and made it my drugs and alcohol. The wrong behaviors can have damaging comfort. There is comfort in crying. The cycle continues and there's the generational curse of not releasing energy and understanding our truth of how we feel in the moment. I did not want my unreleased energy to turn into pain, fear, regret, negative self-talk, lack of forgiveness and drug or alcohol abuse.

The beauty of being able to cry is acknowledging the fact there are tears that come from a good, positive place as well. Crying typically only focuses on pain. We cry when we are happy, excited or have an overwhelming feeling of joy. You still have to be okay with the guilty cry, the ugly cry, the fake cry, the angry cry, the painful cry, the desperate cry, and the cry for help. Cry with an agenda. Be willing to cleanse your spirit, lighten your heart and soul and own what truths you have about crying. I will share my favorite poems with you.

How often do I cry and why?

_____
_____
_____
_____
_____
_____
_____
_____
_____
_____
_____
_____
_____
_____
_____
_____
_____
_____
_____
_____
_____
_____
_____
_____

I beat the odds because I cry when I am releasing energy that brings my tears. I beat the odds because I understand that crying is cleansing. I know crying is another form of expression. I beat the odds because crying is healthy. I cry so others can see the passion in me.

"Why Women Cry"

A little boy asked his mother, "Why are you crying?"

"Because I am a woman," she told him.

"I don't understand," he said.

His mom just hugged him and said, "And you never will."

Later the little boy asked his father, "Why does Mother seem to cry for no reason?"

"All women cry for no reason," was what his dad said.

The little boy grew up and became a man, still wondering why women cry.

Finally he put in a call to God. When God got on the phone, he asked, "God, why do women cry so easily?"

God said, "When I made the woman she had to be special. I made her shoulders strong enough to carry the weight of the world, yet gentle enough to give comfort.

"I gave her an inner strength to endure childbirth and the rejection that many times comes from her children and the world she lives in. I gave her a hardness that allows her to keep going when everyone else gives up, to take care of her family through sickness and fatigue without complaining.

"I gave her the sensitivity to love her children under any and all circumstances, even when her child has hurt her.

"I gave her strength to carry her husband or mate through his faults and fashioned her from his rib to protect his heart.

183

"I gave her wisdom to know that a good husband/man never hurts his wife, but sometimes will test her strength to stand beside him no matter what.

"Finally, I gave her a tear to shed. This is hers exclusively to use whenever it is needed.

"You see, my son," said God, "the beauty of a woman is not in the clothes she wears, the figure she carries, or the way she combs her hair.

"The beauty of a woman must be seen in her eyes, because that is the doorway to her heart, the place where love resides."

God said, "Son, stop asking why,

"It's okay for a woman to cry!"

~Author Unknown

"Men Cry"

The mystery remains for what truly causes men pain. There's so little attention paid to how he takes his pain away.

Men cry silently due to this dreadful world.

Faced with his own pains and he often carries the pains of his favorite girl.

Men cry when they lose all hope. I'd rather see a man cry than hanging from a rope.

Men cry when their dreams get shattered.

 It's that man that refuses to have his woman battered.

Men cry when it seems the world is against them and it's scary.

Men battle with emotions that are often buried.

Men cry when they become extremely frustrated.

You see their smile or smirk, that's how their tears are decorated.

The Bible reflects men have cried through history and throughout time.

Society has made men crying feel like a crime.

Men feel emotions that they hide inside.

They silently cry so they can carry on with their lives.

Men are not made of stone.

Men just cry alone.

Yes, men cry.

Nobody takes the time to find out why.

~Lynne L. Jasames

Final Thoughts

Congrats! You are well on your way to mastering how to *Beat the Odds*!

I wish to emphasize when you are working on a process to becoming better, it is not always about you. Most of the time, we are in so many ways impacting other people. Our behaviors always have and always will impact other people. As you evolve and grow as a person the people around you will either evolve with you or will simply have to leave your circle.

I intentionally and constantly work on developing these ABC's in my own life; some more than others. I beat the odds on a level I never imagined for myself. I pay attention to how each one of these ABC's plays an important part in my growth. I examine if they are not developed because they can hinder my growth. I am constantly working on becoming a better person. If I realize I need to develop a particular value or belief I work on myself in that area.

I shared with you another key factor in how I beat the odds. I've expressed several times I was seventeen years old, had three children and was in foster care. I was determined to finish high school on time with my senior class even though I had no credits at the end of my ninth-grade year. I lived with the constant threat of being separated from my children. I come from a family of addicts and had no role models. I gave you an understanding of when I cried; I used crying as a coping skill to beat the odds.

I am never afraid or hesitant about allowing myself to express myself through my tears. I've been able to bring awareness to other people about the power of tears, the power of crying and the energy crying releases. Crying takes away that built up energy and brings it to the surface to be released.

Allow yourself to believe and inhale everything you have read. Let the ABC's resonate in your thoughts. Now breathe, reflect, and have a good, long, thankful, outrageous, uncontrollable **CRY**. Release the energy of the thoughts and feelings this book evoked. Cry your heart out and cry until you **LAUGH**. Cry for your new changes, your growth and your empowerment to be able to help other people with the right energy behind you.

All it takes is one second for you to lose sight of the things you want to pursue the most in life. One shift in income, family size, health and mindset can set your dreams back for a long time. Get these values and beliefs down on the inside so when you get sidetracked, triggered or life happens they will help you get right back up.

On a final note, I will say meditate. Take time out to breathe and reflect as much as you can. Just breathe. After meditating take the time to listen to God, Spirit, your inner voice and your intuition.

These ABC's will serve a purpose at some point. I want to help prepare you to beat the odds. We all have to face our behaviors with courage and confidence from this day forward.

Change will not come if we wait for some other person or some other time. We are the ones we've been waiting for. We are the change that we seek.

~Barak Obama

You have good days, you have bad days. But the main thing is to grow mentally.

~ Floyd Mayweather Jr.

About the Author

Lynne has over 25 years of professional experience in mentoring, assessing crisis, consulting, training, public speaking, crisis intervention and mental health services in the Las Vegas area. As a Family Services Specialist with Clark County Department of Family Services for over 20 years, Lynne has worked with traumatized at-risk youth and families in crisis. Lynne currently trains prospective foster parents and assists in foster parent recruitment. She uses her speaking, mentoring and training platform to educate incarcerated teen girls and women, individuals, groups and various community organizations on how to beat the odds to achieve a higher level of success, and cope through trauma.

As the author of *It's Okay to Cry When the Odds are Against You*, Lynne provides a unique perspective on overcoming crisis and learning to cope. Lynne earned a bachelor's degree in Sociology (University of Nevada, Las Vegas) and a MBA degree (University of Phoenix). Lynne has a certificate in Crisis Counseling and a certificate in the Seven Domains in Complex Trauma.

Lynne has been featured on the Channel 8 news and was featured in local and other state newspapers. Lynne has been a guest speaker on several radio stations and podcasts to encourage youth and adults to beat the odds.

As the director of the non-profit organization Supporting Underprivileged Americans (SUPA INC), she has collaborated with a multitude of community partners to provide holiday resources, mentoring, backpacks giveaways and other resources to socially disadvantaged families.

When she is not working she enjoys spending time with family and friends as well as reading, running, and laughing.

Made in the USA
Columbia, SC
16 June 2024

36729785R00104